HOT TUB

Mommy

Do All Moms Swear
This Much?

Copyright © 2024 Nicole Lance

**TRAILBLAZER
PUBLISHING**

Trailblazer Publishing

Phoenix, Arizona

www.nicolelance.co

Cover Design & Art: Chani Becker (ChaniBecker.com)

Publishing Alchemist: Heather N. Wilde (HezzieMae.com)

ISBN: 979-8-9871006-2-2

HOT TUB Mommy

Do All Moms Swear This Much?

Nicole Lance

www.nicolelance.co

Other Books By Nicole Lance

Awesome On Your Own Terms: *Intentional Practices to Help You Stop Shoulding and Start Succeeding*

Hot Tub Mommy: *Do All Moms Swear This Much?*

Bold on the Inside: *Amplify Your Impact Without Raising Your Voice* (coming Fall 2024)

Dedication

For Dad. For being that first phone call, and for a million other "Dadvice" sessions since. Thanks for being there. I love you.

Table of Contents

The Adventure Begins

Shit. Shit. Shit.

My stomach dropped and breakfast threatened to reappear as I held that little stick in my hands. "I can't believe this," I muttered out loud. A positive pregnancy test. Followed shortly thereafter by two more because I had to run back to the store to get more tests since the first one was obviously incorrect.

My baby was a surprise. I was in my later thirties when I found out I was pregnant. My stepdaughter was a senior in high school. My husband and I had been together for a decade, and we thought having a baby wasn't in the cards for us. Ever. We were ready to be young empty-nesters, contemplating selling everything and moving to a beach-side studio simply because we had the freedom to do so.

My experiences with babies and kids were minimal. I didn't babysit, and I didn't have younger siblings. I wasn't around a lot of children who were younger than me growing up. I was wholly and completely unequipped and unprepared to have a child. Then, the Universe decided it was going to let me have one of my own. I don't mean to question the cosmos, but what was it thinking?

I didn't have a super clear picture in my head of what life would be like as a mother. I knew it'd be different for sure, but I (perhaps very fortunately) didn't have any idea how different it would be. I thought I'd still be drinking a glass of wine or the occasional martini in the hot tub after putting my daughter to sleep for the night. I mean, we'd still be able to retain some semblance of what life pre-child looked like, wouldn't we?

I laugh now just reading that.

This is not an instructional book. It's not a book about how to become a better mom. It's not a book on parenting styles, how to understand children better, or a prescription for integrating Motherhood, work, and life. It's a collection of stories, and experiences, and reflections of what it's been like to become a mom to this little supernova of a being.

During the process of writing *Hot Tub Mommy*, I found an old collection of typewritten anecdotes that my Mom had captured when I was young. I've included these, too. I lost my Mom five years before my daughter, Emersyn (or Em, as we also call her), was born, so writing about my own daughter and then getting a glimpse into my Mom's perspective, literally in her own words, was a bit magical. Realizing how similar my daughter and I are is simultaneously comforting and terrifying.

This book is for me as much as it is for anyone else. I wanted to attempt to capture the complete hilarity and wonder that is Em. Pretty much since the beginning, I've joked that she has a personality as big as or even bigger than my own. I remind her frequently there's not enough room in our house for the two of us and that I was there first. She cracks me up on a regular basis and challenges me just as often.

I also wanted to write this for myself to remind me that this parenting journey is an iterative, evolving process. There's no roadmap, no advice that will make it all make sense. In fact, it will always be the opposite. Something new to learn, something new to navigate, a new heartbreak, a new unimaginable joy, a new experience that warms the heart, makes me laugh and makes me want to weep at the sheer magnitude of life all at the same time.

I may not be drinking martinis in the hot tub after my little one has (finally) gone to sleep at night like I thought I would, but I am damn grateful to be here with her.

Dear Mom

Dear Mom,

Emersyn just turned six, and we had her kindergarten promotion. I can hardly believe it. Today is her last day of school before summer break. She went on her first horseback ride last week. Her room is always a mess, and no matter how many times I organize them, her dresser drawers always seem to be some mangled explosion of clothing. She's funny and sweet and feels her emotions intensely. (And loudly, most of the time.)

She has nightmares and doesn't like bedtime. She hates the idea of the bath but never wants to leave once she's in it. No matter how cold the pool is, she loves to swim, and skinny-dipping is her current favorite pastime. She's more fearless than I expected she might be. She loves to read books with us, and she's passionate about art. She's incredibly creative, and she loves to have friends over…as long as they play the way she wants them to.

She picked out a "Yoda Best Mom" coffee mug for me for Christmas last year. It's my favorite. She says she wants to be a pop star or a veterinarian (or maybe both) when she grows up. If anyone could figure out how to combine those two things, it would be Em. She'd happily have popsicles and Smarties for breakfast if I let her, and we learned the hard way—more than once—that she'll puke if she eats too many blueberries before bedtime.

I'm afraid she has your sense of rhythm. When she dances, she's completely busting out your moves. It makes me laugh. I saw it for the first time when she was barely sitting up on her own, and her facial expression was so YOU it almost hurt to look at. I'm so grateful to see so much of you in her. She's a giant personality in a tiny package, and according to Dad as well as your friends, she's a carbon copy of me.

I miss you.

I've missed you every step of the way along this journey. I'm sure I always will. I'm so grateful you wrote down your stories from when I was little. Those were such a joy to read. I hope I make half the impact on Emersyn that you did on me.

Wherever you are, I hope you enjoy this.

Love,
Niki

Dear Emersyn

Dear Emersyn,

Mom here. I don't know when or even if you'll ever read this. I hope you do. You'll probably be mad at me for some of the stories I included or for mentioning your current penchant for skinny-dipping. Actually, knowing you, you'll be wondering why it isn't longer. Why I didn't include even MORE stories. I could fill every book in the world with my stories of you. Like I tell you often: you're my favorite human being on the planet.

I love you.

You've brought more to my life than I ever could have imagined. Thank goodness I wasn't able to imagine some of it, in fact! You are the brightest star. You feel big and you love big. I hope you always do.

I'm grateful to be your Mom. I don't anticipate an always-smooth road ahead for both of us. We're too similar for that to be the case. But I do know the foundation of our relationship is strong, and you can be damn sure I'm going to do everything I can to keep it that way.

Thank you for the first six years of this adventure. I'm exhausted and giggling just thinking about it. I miss regular sleep. I've experienced joys far beyond what I knew possible. I've never met such a small being who can instantly skyrocket my blood pressure like you can. It's quite a feat. You crack me up every day, and I hope you never lose that sense of style. You've been turning down my outfit recommendations since you were two years old and insisting on dressing yourself, and I love every one of your combinations. I hope someday you let me brush your hair more often and even let me learn how to French braid it. You probably won't.

I see my mom in you often. Just last night you looked at an old picture and exclaimed, "That's Grandma Sherry!" My heart broke a little. You have her dance moves and sense of rhythm. Sorry about that. You also have her creativity.

I can't wait to see what you do in the world.

Martinis in the hot tub or no, I'm so glad you're here.

Love,
Mom

It's Not Just the Hormones...
I Really Miss Wine

———◆•◆———

"Well, I guess I'm drinking the whole bottle by myself, then!" my friend JoRie exclaimed.

JoRie and our other friend Lisette eyeballed me as I burst into tears after blurting out I was pregnant. Not only was I adjusting to a new self-image as a pregnant person, I missed wine. Outside my immediate circle, these two were the first pair I was announcing my new discovery to. I'd like to blame it solely on the hormones, but the truth was that I really did miss the wine. Mostly, I missed normalcy.

Hell, I still miss normalcy.

Lisette (who we usually refer to as Ted) was pregnant, too, and had just announced it right before me, hence JoRie's solo wine-drinking venture that evening. The difference between me and Ted was that she was excited about being pregnant. For as much as I preach about being intentional in pretty much every area of my life and business, this was a very unintentional circumstance. A very unintentional circumstance with significant outcomes, no less. And I cannot say that—at least at that point in time—I was excited.

This was only one in a series of somewhat bungled pregnancy announcements. I had to warn my dad I was bawling and might be incomprehensible before I called to tell him the news. I was in such a state I was worried he would think some major tragedy had struck or I was actively dying. I had to tell my boss at the time over text message because I knew I wouldn't be able to handle it in the office without being a complete wreck. He was so kind about it that it only made me cry harder.

Then there was the coffee with my long-time friend and colleague, and I'm pretty sure I mangled it enough to say something along the lines of, "Well,

I've screwed up everything at this point," in reference to my career. There was also an incredibly awkward lunch meeting at an out-of-state conference with some colleagues where there was the uncomfortable and highly inappropriate response, "Wonderful, that's what a woman's body was made for!" I sputtered my way through a reply, immediately regretting sharing the news. It wasn't until we enlisted an artistic friend of ours to design a pregnancy announcement that I started to have fun with it. She helped us design something cute to put out on social media and send to friends via text and email, and it was one of the first times I genuinely embraced the announcement.

As the pregnancy went on, I figured out that not only did Em have a penchant for pears (more on that later), but she was a devout reggae fan. I had an hour-long commute throughout my pregnancy, so I had a lot of time to test out her reactions to different genres of music. She didn't react to alternative music, could care less about EDM, and didn't even jam out to some old-school hip hop, much to her dad's chagrin. But put on the reggae channel? My kid was ready to party. To be specific, any time we heard "Three Little Birds" by Bob Marley and the Wailers, she would bop around in my belly, signaling her approval. It's still a favorite of ours, although early on, it had stiff competition from "Elmo's Rap Alphabet" and now runs neck and neck with anything by Taylor Swift. (I'm not sure if she's more into Travis Kelce or Tay-Tay, but I'll take her songs over "Elmo's Rap Alphabet" any day of the week. No offense to Elmo, of course.)

I still missed wine, and I was also finding an amazing new community with other mothers. I felt like I'd found a secret society hiding in plain sight. I was creating a new identity, and I was starting to get an inkling of just how much my life was about to change. It was yet another lesson offered to me by Em that I didn't know I needed.

However, I'm glad that when I hang out with JoRie and Ted now, I'm back to being able to offer my appropriate level of wine-drinking support.

Motherhood's a Gas

If there was a T-shirt that read "Massages give me life," I'd buy one in every color. And I don't mean that in the sense of how lovely it feels to have a stranger oil you up and rub you down. I mean it in the more literal sense of how massages have now become a necessity for basically making my body work properly.

I truly love getting a massage. It was a practice I developed when I was in grad school, and it originally came as a way to help me relax from the tension of balancing a full load of classes, a full-time job, and all the demands of figuring life out as a single person in her early twenties. It was the first time in my life I'd gotten to a financial status where I had a little bit of extra spending money, and there was a local massage place that had a good enough monthly membership deal that I could make it work.

More than twenty years later, I still feel the same way about massages, but the focus of them now is different than it used to be. Up until I became a mom, massages were all about relaxation. Sure, I'd come in with tightness in my shoulders or a tender low back, but it was mostly an opportunity for me to get an hour on the table, de-stress, and think about pretty much whatever I wanted. Sometimes, I would focus on gratitude; sometimes, I would focus on what sort of dreams I wanted to pursue; and sometimes, I would spend my time at the table envisioning having a totally different life. I'd fantasize about new romantic partners, picture the dream house I wanted to live in someday, or I'd create an image of a future professional accomplishment.

Mostly, though, I actually relaxed.

These days, with a rambunctious five-year-old with a personality as giant and as intense as my own running around the house, massages have become a physical necessity. The rock-solid boulders that were once my shoulders need serious maintenance. That tender low back has become a chiropractic and physical therapy issue. Too many hours at the computer have tightened my collarbone and pectoral muscle area to the point of pain. Sitting on the floor for Magna-tiles marathons, board games, and cleaning up endless tiny pieces of plastic toys from various sets and grocery store quarter machines has turned my mid-back into a constant dull ache that quickly morphs into a tight, brittle set of muscles that feel like a frozen rubber band if that area doesn't get regular maintenance. Once pliable enough to prepare for the delivery of a baby, my pelvic and hip muscles turn to cement unless they are lovingly manipulated and intentionally loosened by a skilled massage therapist on a regular basis.

If I'm going to keep up with endless demands for sushi runs, providing my full attention for her latest round of "I want to be a YouTube star" performances, and perching precariously on the toilet while trying to look as interested as possible as she plays a game of "Bathtub Boba Tea Shop" for the hundredth time that week, massages are critical now.

Oh, and those hour-long massages (which are really only ever fifty minutes anyway)? Nope. Give me ninety or give me death! This body needs some serious work.

I'm not blaming my child, per se, though she does present a convenient source of inspiration for these maladies. I mean, it couldn't possibly be the fact that finding time for the gym or a serious yoga session is a puzzle I haven't quite solved. Or that I probably don't drink enough water. Or that I'm working on my laptop too much in places that aren't ergonomically correct. Or that I fall asleep at least twice a week with my head and neck at an awkward angle on the side of her pillow as I'm helping her fall asleep.

Regardless of what's driving the need for these massages, they are a line item in my monthly budget that has moved from the luxury desire column into the basic necessity column, and I try to resource myself with them on a regular basis.

One time, however, it had been a few months between appointments. Work had been wild, life had been life-y, and I was desperate. In an odd way, the Universe might have intervened via my desperation to save me from the embarrassment of this particular appointment because my two favorite therapists were already booked, and I could not wait one more day, let alone another week, until Frank or Ryan had openings. A lovely young woman greeted me when it was time for my appointment, and after she left me to get ready, I wasted no time stripping down and hopping face-first on that lovely, warm table. I nestled my face into the little hole and felt my body start relaxing. I'm pretty sure I have a Pavlovian reaction at this point to laying on a massage table like that, and the anticipation of muscle release and relaxation made me almost giddy.

The session started, and I relaxed further as my muscles released. I started to zone out a bit- moving into a Zen-like state of semi-meditative relaxation. I was thrilled to notice my brain wasn't whirling with grocery and meal planning and holiday plans and work to-do lists. Holy hell. I was feeling a little sleepy. Maybe I could just slide a bit further into that pre-sleep state. I didn't want to snore and embarrass myself or anything, and I could tell I was getting close. I'd caught myself right on the edge of what I would call a "pre-snore" and had rescued it right at the last minute.

Little did I know snoring was the least of my concerns.

Whether it was the magic in those warm little mitts of my masseuse as she rubbed in some CBD oil, the calming music softly being piped in through the vents, the gentle warmth of the massage table below me, or the sheer exhaustion of running at an unsustainable pace for far too long, I'll never know, but I dropped into full sleep.

My own fart woke me up.

I freaking farted. In front of a human I didn't know. While I was naked and covered only by a thin cloth sheet. While she was rubbing my body. It wasn't a juicy exclamation of a ripper, at least, perhaps more aptly described as a polite little toot. Maybe even just a "pfft" if I'm being honest.

But it was enough.

Even writing this now, I'm dying inside. In the multiple decades I'd been getting massages, this was never a bridge I had to cross. Although, as I'm reflecting on this now in all its re-lived horror glory, I'm starting to wonder if it had ever happened before and I'd slept through it. Fuck. That thought will keep me up at night!

It was all I could do to stay on the table. I wanted to grab my clothes and bolt for the door, but I also knew I wanted to be able to come back someday. I immediately started apologizing profusely while simultaneously thanking whatever gods of massage may exist that I didn't have to look her in the eye. I made a pathetic, bumbling attempt at a compliment of how I was so relaxed I let one slip, but I could tell I was making it worse for both of us. She gave a sort of half-laugh and told me I wasn't the first client to pass gas during a massage, and I'm not sure that made me feel any better.

I did my best to relax—but not too much—for the remainder of the time, keeping my eyes firmly closed to avoid all eye contact when I was asked to roll over on my back. I've never gotten dressed so fast and left a tip so quickly at any massage experience in the rest of my life.

I'm pretty sure my kid is to blame for this, too.

On Travel...

———◆•◆———

I love to travel alone. I love bringing a book to a bar or restaurant in a new city. I love booking a nice hotel room with a good view and a big bathtub. I love to get to the airport early so I can enjoy an overpriced drink or two before boarding. I research yummy places to eat and love to drive around my new location before settling in for the evening. I love to book extra time on business trips so I can relax, rest, read, walk on the beach, or do something fun the locals recommend.

When I was pregnant, I pictured future me still doing these things. Moms need to relax, too, right? A business trip could serve a dual purpose—its original, work-oriented function and also an escape—a little solo mommy getaway to recharge and get back to some of my pre-baby ways.

I underestimated how much this would shift, too. I still feel all of those things I used to feel, but there's another feeling layered in there now. A little bit of hollowness often underlies the experience now. I'm not always as excited about booking extra time away. (On the flip side, sometimes I'm like, "Thank fuck, I'm getting away this week." I feel a tinge of guilt at leaving Sean behind on the front lines, but I'm getting pretty good at releasing that feeling quickly!)

The first time I drafted this section, I was getting ready to head out on a business trip for two nights. Here's what I wrote:

"We have been going nonstop since school started, and fall break is just around the corner. We've got four more days of school, and then she's off for a little over two weeks because she's on a modified year-round schedule. This year, I have committed to spending the entire fall break with her, with the exception of two nights when I'll be gone for one speaking engagement

I have at an international conference in Austin, Texas. I intentionally kept the time unscheduled so I could focus on Emersyn, go on adventures with her, and just live life in general a bit without the specter of work looming in the background. I literally know in my heart and in my head that I'm about to be spending 24/7 with her for two full weeks, and yet I'm still feeling a little sad and maybe even a little guilty about this business trip I'm about to go on today! If I were to step outside of myself, I would be yelling at me, 'Don't be ridiculous! Enjoy the time! You're going to need it to get you through the two weeks! Listen to what you want on the radio while you drive! Take up all the space in the bed! Enjoy the silence!'

And while, yes, I felt and often still feel all of those things, I also feel like I want to be with my daughter. Not just out of an overblown sense of duty or the cultural pressures to experience 'Mom guilt,' but out of a genuine sense that at this point in my life, my primary place in the world is with Em. This can create a distracting conundrum when traveling. I am always intentionally present for my clients and audiences, but I want to show up for myself, too. Give me some of that nurturing and nourishing that I so often offer to others but perennially find in short supply for myself."

Fast forward a few months, and I'm in Colorado for a speaking engagement. As I re-read what I previously wrote, I know that was true for me then. Sometimes it's still true for me now.

Not on this trip, though, baby! I needed to be here for two nights for a speaking engagement, but since one of my favorite humans in the world lives in Colorado and was going to be at the conference, we decided to book an extra night to get some downtime and are going to be soaking in some natural hot springs all day tomorrow, talking incessantly, probably eating dinner in our jammies in the hotel room, and having a luxuriously unrushed Saturday morning before my afternoon flight.

Do I feel guilty? Not really.

I mean, guilt crossed my mind a time or two, but it's more like a longing to know that my kiddo is ok and maybe feeling a bit bad that my partner is shouldering all the responsibility with her while I get to play in the mountains for a few days. And if I investigate those feelings a bit further, there's not a lot of depth. This is normal for us. It's healthy for their relationship. Hell, it's healthy for my marriage. A little distance, some experiential empathy, a lot of processing, and restorative time for me. Some awesome cocktails, a king-sized bed to myself, no one but me to take care of, and I can come home feeling full and ready to re-engage.

Nothing to feel guilty about there.

My mom must have had an infinite number of opportunities to capture snippets of hilarious conversations and sayings from my childhood. Between me and my brother and our conversations together, I'm sure she had enough material. I love that she recorded some of these.

FAMOUS QUOTATIONS FROM NICKIE

(Age 4)

1. Mom, I went to the bathroom in the back yard, but let's not tell Dad because he'll just get all furrustrated and mad, okay?

2. If you don't let me go with you Mom, I'll cry pure ashes from eyes!!!

3. Wow, man, this is really rad!!

4. (Talking to Grandma on the phone) Well, we don't have a lot of things. Like, we don't have a pool or anything, just because of my dumb old Mom.

5. My feelin's are hurt! They're really hurt! All because you called me a rat! my feelin's will actually be hurt forever!!

6. Well, Mom, that's certainly not right. You certainly should know how to do it better than that!

Crotch-roaches, Certitude, and Skepticism

"Mom, Santa's not even real, is he?"

At only three years old, Em was well ahead of my imagined schedule of when I would have to answer certain questions. I'm not a big "perpetuate the myth of Santa Claus and then admit it was all a lie when they're older" kind of person, but I was hoping my kiddo might enjoy a few solid years of childhood magic before we started dismantling some of her childhood illusions.

Not wanting to lie to her, I fumbled out something about the magic of Santa and the holiday spirit, and then I asked her what she thought. She glanced out her window, gave her signature Emersyn shoulder shrug, and said, "Nah." I asked if she still wanted to go to the store for Christmas lights and holiday inflatables for the front yard, and she responded with an enthusiastic "Yeah!" and threw her hands in the air.

A few years before Em was born, I started buying those holiday inflatable decorations for the front yard. It started off like any addiction: affordable, manageable, and not over the top. Also, like any addiction, it has gotten out of control and morphed into an annual event that now requires detailed planning. I even had a hand-drawn layout and spreadsheet this last year to help me figure out how to put everything together. Since Em entered the picture, she has become more involved with the annual planning for our holiday yard. Like a tiny General preparing for battle, she gets a serious face any time we talk about it. It doesn't matter if it's wintry unicorns or happy holiday gnomes; each potential addition gets serious consideration.

Of course, she's also got no concept of budget, so she only wants the special edition *Star Wars* inflatables or the absolutely giant blow-ups that can be synchronized to music. She has no regard for the fact that our front yard is pretty small, and we're basically limited to the ones seven and a half feet in size, max. Last year she was pissed that Lowe's didn't have her preferred selection. I'm pretty sure if she could have, she would have taken over the Store Manager's job and dictated inventory orders. Hell, knowing her, she probably would have done alright with it, too.

I hoped my Santa-related redirection worked and we could coast from there, except that's not how my kid works. She operates with certitude, whether it's warranted or not. It wasn't just that holiday season that we received inquiries about Santa. It's been every single year since. This past season, in kindergarten, I was a bit concerned that her skepticism might splash over onto her classmates and ruin some magic for them, so we had a bit of a conversation around, "You know, Em, other kids believe lots of different things about Santa, and some kids don't celebrate Christmas at all or don't have money for Santa to help bring presents, so we need to be a bit careful how we talk about this to make sure we're being respectful of everyone's situations." It might have been a lot to take in, but my kiddo usually gets it. As I've been on the receiving end of already far more than I expected, I got Em's signature "My mom's an idiot" look. She assured me she was aware of the dynamics and able to navigate them.

Sheesh.

For a small human who still gets an awful lot of things wrong, Em doesn't hesitate to express her certainty. In fact, since she was about eighteen months old, Sean and I have posited that Em has a fierce inner monologue where she actually ends every sentence in her own head with, "...you dumb fuck." As in, "Yes, Mommy, I know it's almost time for bath...you dumb fuck." Or, "Sure, Daddy, I'll put my toys away when I'm done...you dumb fuck." It might be funnier or more endearing if it wasn't aimed directly at us.

Her conviction and confidence also lend themselves to her vocabulary and pronunciation of words. Like adding an extra 'd' to the end of the word human so it's pronounced "humand" and also to her middle name so she calls herself "Emersyn Cheryld Lance" instead of just Cheryl. My mom's name was Cheryl, so I'm sure she's getting a kick out of that one. Here in Arizona, there's a gorgeous part of the state called Chino Valley. Em promptly translated that into Cheeto Valley. Of course there's the fan favorite "scabetti" or "Scabetti-O's" instead of spaghetti, and my personal favorite: crotch-roaches instead of cockroaches. This has become a regular word among our family and friends, complete with an emoji to go with it. (Seriously, who invented the giant cockroach emoji with a huge heart on it??)

However, there was one word that took us a few days—and a few "frustrated Em" tantrums to figure out: Beeoggus. Pronounced Bee-YOG-Uss, with an emphasis on the 'yog.' There was a week-long period when Em was about two years old where she walked around repeating this word. Occasionally, she would look around the house for something, complaining that she couldn't find Beeoggus. It sounded more like a villain in a child's storybook than something that would be desired by a toddler, and neither Sean nor I could figure it out.

Then came the fateful night she threw an absolutely epic tantrum as we were trying to leave the house to go out to dinner. She stomped around the house in a panic because she couldn't find her Beeoggus. We all looked, offering suggestions and desperately praying we would magically find it, even though we had no idea what we were looking for. To no avail, we decided to move the tantrum into the car, hoping the change of scenery would eventually tone her down. Imagine our surprise when we wrench open the back door to get her into the car seat, and she suddenly shouts, "BEEOGGUS!"

"No fucking way," Sean muttered with all the frustration and cynicism any parent who's ever wasted minutes of their life in a fruitless search for a child's lost toy that wouldn't have been lost if only they'd listened to you about putting it away in the first place has ever experienced. He hung onto

Em while she squirmed around for something on the floorboard of the car. She proceeded to hand him a plastic toy version of Lumiere, the talking, singing, and dancing candelabra from Disney's movie *Beauty and the Beast*. At that point, still red-faced but now smiling and laughing, Em was totally placated and happily allowed her father to buckle her into the car seat. I looked at her and said, "Em, I don't get it. THAT is the Beeoggus?" She nodded enthusiastically as she pushed the button on the base of the toy, and it started to sing.

"Be. Our. Guest." You know the song from the movie that goes, "Be our guest, be our guest, put our service to the test…" Well, those first three words are sung in a bit of a French accent and are spaced apart with little pauses in between, so to her little ears and brain, "Be our guest" sounded exactly like: BEEOGGUS. Mystery solved.

There's also another quality that Emersyn displays that I simultaneously hope she never loses and also pray she learns to leverage appropriately: she pulls absolutely zero punches and is a direct communicator. When it comes to things like what she wants to wear, what she wants to eat, or what she wants to do, this is a great thing. It can be a pain in the ass when we're on opposing sides, but I always appreciate that she knows her own desires and isn't afraid to communicate them. Sometimes, however, a bit more empathy and tact might be appreciated.

One afternoon, I was having a bit of a moment, missing my mom. I keep a framed photo of her in our living room on the bookcase, and as Em was playing, she had done something that made me think of my Mom. I went over and grabbed the photo and turned to Emersyn and said, "You know who absolutely would have loved what you just did and who would have loved you like crazy? Grandma Sherry." Like I said, I was having a bit of a moment, so my eyes were a little teary and my voice caught. It felt tender and sweet. Then Em responded.

"Yeah, but she's dead, Mommy."

Em was not wrong. She sure was. Thanks for the reminder, kid.

Along the same lines of death and understanding how things work, Em went through a phase where this was a larger part of the conversation than perhaps Sean or I bargained for. Somehow Em and I got on the topic of what she wanted to do after high school, whether she wanted to go to college, join the Navy like her sissy, become a fighter pilot like her Uncle Ponch, or whether or not she'd become a world-famous pop star. She also suggested becoming a YouTube star, but since she keeps encouraging people to "describe" in the comments below instead of "subscribe," that may not be quite as viable of a future career. I suppose time will tell. We started talking about other far in the future things, like her getting married and maybe having kids someday. She paused for a moment and then said, "You'll be dead by then, right?"

Talk about a buzzkill. Again, she may not be wrong, but I really wasn't ready for the reminder of my own mortality in the midst of all these exciting future scenarios.

However, one of my very favorite aspects of her personality is the ultimate confidence she has in herself. One night in kindergarten, she and I were home on a Friday night and painting together. She stopped painting and slowly placed her brush on the table, then made sure I was making full eye contact before she said, "Mom, this is kind of scary to say…" She then dramatically put her hands on her head and placed her elbows on the table. At this point, I'm all in, 100% emotionally invested. It was a major mom moment! My child had articulated she's frightened of something! Time to activate the emotionally present parenting skills! I was receptive! I was calm! I was fully engaged! After a brief encouragement to share and reassuring her that she could tell me anything and that I was wholeheartedly listening to her, she took a big breath, blew it out with closed eyes, and then turned to me. "Well, I think I just might be the very best designer ever, like in the whole entire world." She looked pointedly at her painting as if to drive home the significance of her statement.

All I could do was agree, with total solemnity, it did in fact appear to be true that she was the best designer ever, like in the whole entire world.

Sure, I'll Just Schedule My Emotional Needs for Later

I've been with my partner for over a decade and a half, and one of the things we had to learn about each other was that while I will shoot out of bed like a fireball, in full possession of my mental faculties, with my to-do list and strategic approach to the day whirring through my brain, solving ten problems, answering texts, and sending an email all while waiting for the coffee to brew, he…doesn't. In fact, optimal wind-up time for my partner is a solid ninety minutes, a little over half a pot of coffee, and zero verbal interruptions.

Of course, with a little one at home, that's not always possible, but for the good of the household and the well-being of our marriage, I do what I can to make this happen. I've become accustomed to writing a list of questions to ask when he's more awake and withholding some of the input I'm just dying to share as I thought over our "discussion" from the night before. (a.k.a. all the things I wished I'd said but didn't think of that are now top of mind because I got to sleep a little. I was also able to ruminate on the conversation around 2 a.m., and now that I'm awake and have my proverbial engines fully revved, I'm ready to re-engage.)

All in all, the pause-and-wait strategy has been helpful. I get answers from a human who is more fully engaged with the world around him, and he gets to start the day the way he'd prefer. It's a win-win, and with rare exceptions, we make it work. It took me a while to acclimate to the approach because I wanted my emotional needs met when I wanted them met, dammit! I didn't want to wait another hour and a half. I was ready to talk NOW. Over time, however, I realized it wasn't about not getting my needs met at all; it was more of a matter of when. And most of the time, another hour or so wasn't too much of a wait in the grand scheme of things.

When we had our baby, however, I was wholly unprepared for the number of times I would need to schedule time later for having my emotional needs met. I'm not talking about waiting an hour or so for a break so I could process what needed to be processed, either. I'm talking about being so busy and consumed with taking care of another being that your own needs might have to wait a few days until there's time and space for them. Call it selfishness, call it naivete, call it what you will, but I was not ready for a world in which I would have to do so much "wait and process later."

Emersyn ricochets from one emotion to the next like a pinball that's been shot out of a high-powered rifle instead of merely whacked with one of the little flippers inside the game.

Similar to how my husband wakes up, I don't entirely pivot as quickly as she does. I need some time to work through my own emotions when there's been something intense. When Emmy is having a hard time, or a "big feeling cycle," as the amazing parenting coach Darlynn Childress calls it, I try hard to stay with her. I do my best to help her process her feelings, recognize the emotions, and move that energy through her body. The challenge is by the time she's done with her cycle, I'm still locked in the initial stages of my own. Emersyn, of course, is ready to move on to what's next, and I need to move on as well in order to keep up with her.

This often results in me not having the time I need or the time I want to process events in real time. It's hard to go back and process my own pissed-off-ness when my little one is standing in front of me, fully recovered and ready for a popsicle. So, like many things, I bottle it up—sometimes neatly, sometimes not so neatly—and store it away, wanting to be present and supportive and to give her a clear emotional environment in which to operate.

In this way, she's an excellent teacher. She rode through her cycle, expressed her emotions, and is now moving on to something more fun and enjoyable. I would love to learn to do that better! The challenge is taking the time to do it and not forsaking it in light of the myriad of other things crowding my plate and calling for my attention. This doesn't mean I stuff away all my emotional processing and present a completely false front. There are plenty of times when I share with her, "Mommy's still resetting from the beginning of this situation when you were kicking and screaming on the floor while yelling about how I'm the meanest, and you're so mad, and all you wanted to do was watch TV."

Most of the time she kind of looks at me like I'm an idiot for hanging on to something that's so obviously over. Maybe I am hanging onto it too long. Maybe I'm honoring a process I need to follow. Maybe if I give myself a little bit of grace here, I can also see that I'm doing the best I can and am still learning.

Processing my own feelings while navigating a child's emotional rollercoaster is one thing, but when it's a matter of physical illness as opposed to emotional disruption, the whole game changes. Becoming indisposed is simply not an option.

Forget drinking martinis in a hot tub; I want to be able to sip ginger ale on the couch through a bendy straw and watch trash TV while I heal. The fact that tiny humans don't give a shit about how you're feeling perhaps shouldn't be as big of a surprise as it has been to me, but even now, as I'm writing this and Emersyn is five years old, I'm still shocked at how hard it is to get space to take care of myself when I get sick. And that's writing from someone who has the privilege of being partnered with another full-bodied, allegedly completely capable adult!

Emersyn's recognition of when I'm sick goes something like this, "Oh, yeah, Mommy's sick. I'm sorry you're sick, Mommy. Hey, can I have...?" and then she inserts multiple iterations of demands and needs that must be met, preferably immediately, and definitely involving popsicles, any sort of paint that will create a huge mess, something with glitter, or a random request to adopt a cat because she senses my defenses are low. At this point I at least feel vindicated that there is some acknowledgment I'm not feeling well. In her younger years, there was a vague sense of confusion that would cross her face as she tried to process the fact I could possibly not be in a state to simply exist only to meet her every request as quickly as possible.

I was in the bathroom experiencing some physical symptoms of illness, the likes of which I will spare readers the description of, and the door burst open. "MOM. I NEED YOU." I don't even remember what the critical need of the moment was. A Barbie that needed a jacket replaced (which is nearly impossible because of the shape of their hands, the narrowness of those tiny little sleeves, and the bajillion loose threads that get caught on their little Barbie fingers as you try to maneuver their arms through), a lemonade that needed to be refilled, a snack that couldn't be reached…it doesn't matter what it was in terms of the tangible thing she needed.

I was reminded yet again what a rollercoaster parenthood is and also how absolutely fortunate I am to be healthy most of the time. This, in turn, prompted an even deeper reflection on the bonds and connections to other mothers that I now feel.

I thought of the parents out there who didn't have a partner and who were sick and still needed to take care of the little ones. Those who don't have access to medicine, nutritious foods, and medical care or paid time off from work to rest and heal. I felt immensely appreciative and in awe of the amount of support I really did have.

I still miss pooping alone, though.

Mornings

I used to love mornings.

Sometimes, I long for the days I lived alone. For a slow, solo morning to lay around in bed and half-dream, with enough time to meditate in a calm, centered, healing space and then to journal, plan the day, do yoga…

I don't know that I ever even really had that type of morning. If I did, it certainly wasn't with any outstanding amount of regularity, but that's the picture I have in my head when I compare my desires to current reality. Mostly, I want a morning where I get to wake up, be unrushed, and not have to get back up off the couch sixteen times to get my kid a lemonade, a yogurt, some fruit, and then have to open the popsicle wrapper. (Because hell, yes, I let her have popsicles for breakfast most weekends.)

It's not so much that I truly want to live alone again, although I still have some pretty vivid fantasies about that occasionally. It's more that I sometimes long for mornings that have that sort of spaciousness instead of the little hands tapping the mattress or the side of my face and asking if it's time to wake up, can I please watch TV, and can you get me a drink and a blanket?

There are some benefits to being the chosen parent to wake up first thing in the morning, though—the snuggles are usually pretty good and Emersyn's hair still smells yummy like shampoo and not like little kid sweat and playground ick. Tempers are most often sweeter than later in the day, too. And even when the request is for pre-dawn arts and crafts or book reading, there's usually enough warmth in the connection to melt my resistance or any residual frustration about the lost relaxation time under my covers.

But some mornings, like this morning, there's a small (ok, maybe not so small) part of me that is frustrated and resentful. Remembering that two dissimilar things can both exist, I'm also consciously grateful for my little one and acknowledging the beauty of this moment under a fuzzy blanket on the couch while a cartoon movie plays perhaps a little too loudly on the TV. In addition to that, however, is the part of me that wishes I were alone right now with a candle, my journal, and some sage smoke going, mapping out a day that was unlikely to include acting out highly dramatic tales with Barbies or fishing small bath toys out before they got sucked down the drain during the pre-bedtime rituals.

I've learned to appease that part of me when and where I can—offering her some moments of solitude even though I can't get her the hours of silence and alone-ness she sometimes craves. I sit on the couch, coffee precariously balanced to the left, headphones firmly situated on my head with a white noise app playing sounds of pouring rain and crashing ocean waves, trying to meditate or at least connect with myself long enough to write these few paragraphs. To my right is my daughter, cuddled up under a soft blanket because although she refuses to wear socks, long sleeves, or pants and avows with all the certainty and cockiness she can pack into her little body that she is, in fact, NOT cold…she is indeed chilly. Her head is on my shoulder, both arms wrapped around my right arm, increasing the difficulty level of trying to type. She's squirmy, twisting around, trying to touch my computer, and I can feel her energy level rising to what will soon feed the burst that will propel her off the couch and into the first of many, many, many activities throughout the day.

"Both can exist" runs through my mind like a mantra. I can both love sitting here with her and also desire a morning that doesn't include this motherhood balancing act.

Ranch Dressing Tsunamis

School lunches: I feel like I've entered a new level of hell.

First of all, I did not know there were thousands of online videos of people making incredibly artistic and extremely complicated school lunches allegedly for children. Based on the fact these people a) have time to do this and b) are actively and intentionally perpetuating a myth that a grade school child's lunch should have a theme and include hand-created artistic elements in support of that theme, I can only assume they actually do not have children and actually are not responsible for feeding them and for getting them to school in a timely fashion. My daughter stumbled upon these videos a month or so before kindergarten started, and I can assure you that what she's taking to school looks nothing like the uber-cute Super Mario Brothers or Star Wars-themed and color-coordinated bento-box style lunches these alleged other kids allegedly have.

In fact, I've become one of the school district lunch program's staunchest advocates. I consider myself their unofficial hype woman each week as I read the menu to Em. "Ooh! Nachos! Oh, heck yes, spaghetti! Ah, man, you can get cucumber slices, too?! WHOA!" as I dance around enthusiastically to signal my support of these menu options. Em is predictably unimpressed unless it's pizza day.

Second of all, we need to talk about the tiny containers.

All. The. Tiny. Containers. There are mini containers for dressings and dips, mini containers so your berries don't get squished, mini containers for pretzels. And, of course, you have to make sure those tiny little fingers are capable of opening those tiny little containers, so they have to be the ones with the lids that are easy enough to remove. That means these containers typically don't completely close properly, and that ranch dressing you painstakingly portioned out in hopes it would actively encourage your child to eat the cucumbers in their lunch that you so lovingly sliced and put into the other tiny container will now slosh around the lunchbox in a tsunami of dairy-based motherly love that said mother (or partner, if present and willing) will later have to clean out. Oh, and all those other little tiny containers will be covered in it, too.

Sigh.

Third, we need to talk about the washing and care and upkeep of these things. When we first started, I was determined we didn't need an army of these tiny-ass containers under the cupboard. It was already overflowing with old blender bottles, water bottles, insulated to-go coffee cups, and a well-intentioned but poorly implemented lid organization system. This was the cabinet I dreaded opening. I didn't want to add a million tiny containers to it and a million and a half tiny lids (because somehow they multiply, but the containers stay the same). I figured we would just unpack the lunchbox, clean out the containers, and reuse them for the next day.

I highly underestimated the amount of work it is just to clean out the damn lunchbox itself, sort through the remains of what got eaten, what didn't get eaten, and figure out what the hell the slimy thing in the corner was or was not. Not to mention the ranch tsunami clean-up efforts. And oh yeah, all of this is occurring while you have a kindergartener bouncing around, asking for a snack while you're trying to prepare dinner because the school pick-up time is right in that awkward hour where if they have a snack, they won't eat dinner, but if you don't give them a snack you will have an unbearably cute but enraged whining monster on your hands until dinner is finally ready, but damn it's hard to get dinner ready when you're also trying to clean out this fucking lunchbox.

Whew.

Perhaps veteran parents are shaking their heads at me right now, and perhaps I will someday, too. Maybe I'll get my feet firmly planted under me, and one of those seemingly elusive but oh-so-predictable routines will emerge that will make everything smoother and easier. I'll find the exact right containers that are easy to open but don't spill, and we'll bump into the exact right lunch components which will mean my daughter comes home with a happily full tummy. She'll enjoy packing lunches with me and will be ready and willing to do so immediately when I ask.

Yeah, right.

It was interesting to discover my mom struggled to get me to sleep, much in the same way we have struggled with Emersyn. We'll have to try this technique!

Conversations with Nickie

Nick: Mom, I can't sleep!!

Mom: Close your eyes and think of your very favorite thing in the whole world.

Nick: Hmmmm. Encanto Park!!

Mom: Nicole--your very favorite thing in the whole world is NOT your mother? It's a lousy park?

Nick: Yep.

Mom: C'mon, Nicole, what's your favorite thing, really?

Nick: I told you--the park!

Mom: Nicole!

Nick: Okay!! Encanto Park and Mom.

Mom: Thanks Nick. You have a big heart. Now what's your next favorite thing?

Nick: The beach!

Mom: Next?

Nick: School!

Mom: Next?

Nick: Daddy!!!

Mom: Next?

Nick: Ian!

Mom: Next?

Nick: Miss Lynn and Miss Lois.

Mom: How about Otter Pops? Aren't they in the top ten?

Nick: Nope. My friends are next. Then Otter Pops. Then Chips Ahoy.

Mom: Now close your eyes and think of each one of these special things verrrrrry slowly, and the next thing you know it'll be morning!

Nick: I know how this goes. If you close your eyes, these things show up and you have them all, all at once. It's called dreaming. I did that once. Can I dream an Otter Pop? I'm hungry.

Mom: Sure. You can dream anything, but you have to go to sleep. Now close your eyes!

Nick: Can I pretend I'm a baby again? Why don't we have another baby?

Unrushed

I have almost forgotten what it is like to not be driven by someone else's schedule. To not be rushed. To not be worried about a tiny human's snack, sleep, bathing, or pooping schedule. To not have my head on a swivel, keeping an eye out for an easily accessible restroom (even though my still somewhat newly-minted motherhood bladder might recommend otherwise, for no one else's sake but my own). To not be pulling up Google Maps incessantly, making sure kid-friendly food or snack options are readily available in case "hanger" strikes.

I'm writing this right now while in California on a solo weekend. My plans include sleep, writing, reading, and disconnecting from the usual frenzied pace and relentless "giving to others" that tends to be my standard operating procedure. I left home about six hours ago after a morning that included three outfit changes for Emersyn because I clearly wasn't keeping appropriate tabs on my child's change in fashion preferences; multiple refusals to let me even brush her hair followed shortly thereafter by asking her dad, *right in front of me no less,* to put in a ponytail, and negotiating at Jimmy Hoffa-level proficiency to not brush her teeth. I've negotiated with police unions that were easier to work with than my kid when she doesn't want to brush her teeth.

I took a meeting in the airport, set my out-of-office email response, flew to Cali, grabbed a rental car, and managed to set the phone to work properly with the car's Bluetooth system AND oriented all of the mirrors correctly. I still feel like a spring that's uncoiling. In re-reading that, well, no shit. No wonder I'm still feeling like I'm ready to spring into action.

I'm in a tiny coastal town I'd never heard of, tasting a flight of beer samples at a brewery I've never heard of, either. No one knows me here. I don't owe anyone anything. They have a record player and are playing one of my all-time favorite songs by one of my all-time favorite bands. I'm trying to get my body to get the memo my spirit has been trying to send—to recalibrate to being *unrushed*. Even just the word itself makes me relax when I think about it. Unrushed. Not going a million miles an hour. I have time to sit and experience and soak it in if I want to. Marinate, even. Nobody needs me, and I am not beholden to any calendar except the requests of my own body and prompts of my intuition.

I have no idea what the hell I'm going to do for the next two days!

Have I ever been unrushed before? Maybe I'm associating this relentless sense of busyness, and over-responsibility, and pervasive exhaustion with motherhood unfairly. Maybe this isn't to be blamed solely on my little one or my parenting naivete. What if this is just my personality? Or if not my personality, what if it's just an approach to navigating life that I've adopted and embodied for so long I've forgotten it's possible to experience my days otherwise? (Or maybe never knew it was possible!) What if I've simply swapped out things like ambition or caretaking for my kid as an excuse and reason to be rushing around all the time?

What if it's possible to be the kick-ass mom I want to be without being constantly on the run?

I wrote the first part of this chapter about nine months ago, and I decided to let it sit. Then I let it sit some more. I went back and re-read it and allowed myself to look at it without the usual judgment with which I approach self-reflections like that. I meditated on it. I journaled on it.

This is the thing about kids. At least, it's the thing about me and my kid. I am constantly in awe of what she prompts for me in terms of self-growth. Whether it's interacting with her directly, trying to figure out how to interact with her directly, or trying to get the hell away from her for a break for a bit, she is a constant spurrer-on of my spiritual and emotional growth and development.

This little musing on my trip kicked off a months-long journey that I'm still experiencing. I've taken a hard look at some of my habits, gotten extensive coaching, and meditated and self-reflected my ass off. I've delved deep into the roots of my productivity addiction and recalibrated how I want to show up for others as well as for myself. There have been a lot of tears, and there have been a ton of triumphs. Mostly, I thought about whether or not I was showing Emersyn a way to live that might be something she'd like to experience someday. Was I demonstrating a way of approaching life that was values-led, fulfilling, and choice-driven? Was I dealing with past traumas and experiences in a healthy way that let me steer my own approach to life? Hell, was I living life in a way that I truly wanted to?

It was a lot. It's still a lot. I imagine it will always be a lot. I'm good with that. I want to live a life that's a lot, and I want my daughter to live a life that's exactly how she wants it, too.

I wonder if I could ever have seen this for myself without her.

Fingus, Pickle Cheese, and the Art of Reinvention

---•◆•---

When Em came home from her first week of the freshly started preschool year with stories of her new friend Fingus, Sean and I were certain she had the name wrong. We asked her repeatedly if she was sure she was pronouncing their name correctly and if that was also how the teachers pronounced it. Increasingly insistent that the child's name was actually Fingus, we decided to let it go. After all, we were at a private Montessori school where some of the kids had truly unique names. We went to each school event and classroom get-together eagerly hoping to meet the much-lauded Fingus, but no such luck.

Throughout the year, Sean and I made a point of checking in to see if good old "Fingus" was still around. Em assured us he was. Finally, at the end of the year party, there was a family we hadn't crossed paths with. The parents introduced themselves and then their son, Felix. Emmy triumphantly looked at us and said, "See?! This is who I've been talking about!" "This is Fingus?" I blurted. Em nodded vigorously. Before the parents could give me too weird of a look, I introduced myself to Felix, made small talk for a bit with the parents as I explained the year-long mispronunciation, and tried to hold in my laughter. I could see the glee in Sean's eyes as we finally solved the mystery of Fingus.

Kid pronunciations are the best. Equally as entertaining was the day Em came home from kindergarten and shared with me the names of her new friends in class. She started listing off names like Gabby, Gracelyn, Pickle Cheese, Nash… "Hold up, Em. Go back one. Did you just say Pickle Juice?" With an eye roll that makes me shudder in anticipation of her teen years, she replied in a tone befitting my obviously low intellect, "No, Mom. I said Pickle Cheese. CHEESE. Not Juice." (...you dumb fuck.)

Oh, well, that explained it all! I inquired a bit further because although I was willing to perhaps consider that a set of well-intentioned parents may name their child Fingus, I couldn't quite wrap my head around Pickle Cheese as a moniker for a cute, snuggly, squishy little baby. Thankfully, there was an explanation for this one. Em shared that her classmate, whose real name was James, didn't like his name and wanted to choose something else, so he decided on "Pickle Cheese." It's kind of hard to argue with a kindergartener who's looking to reinvent himself, so I shrugged and said, "Cool," and we moved on to the next thing.

It did get my wheels turning a bit, though. It seemed so clear-cut to these kids that if they didn't like something, they could simply change it and do so without great fanfare or drama. There was no need to justify the name and no questioning of it on Em's behalf. It simply was, and she was willing to respect that.

Why the heck do we, as adults, overcomplicate this so much?

Oreo 2.0

As an executive coach, I work a lot with guilt—my own and other people's. I'm not surprised when requests for time, needing to reschedule, or even the rare sick day leave me or my clients feeling guilt-ridden and questioning my value as a human on planet Earth. However, I was entirely unprepared for and caught off guard by the level of guilt that a one-inch fish in a ten-gallon tank has generated.

My daughter has wanted a cat "ever since she was a little kid," according to her. (At the time I wrote this, she was only five, remember.) Dad is not a fan of cats, and we tried adopting a dog that wasn't a great fit and it reminded me of just how much time I absolutely do not have to be taking care of a four-legged family member who requires attention and exercise. I can't even manage to give myself those two things since becoming a mom!

Em's facial expressions are sadder than a Sarah McLachlan commercial soundtrack when she talks about wanting a pet. She asked about getting a fish tank one day, and either in a rare burst of overestimating my personal time and capacity or an episode of my brain and mouth being temporarily hijacked by aquarium-loving aliens, I said yes.

Now, one of the other things I did not know about becoming a parent was that these tiny humans have minds like steel traps and will remember exactly where you were standing, what was going on around you, and the verbatim words you used to make any sort of promise. It could be as simple as letting them have extra bubble bath in the bathtub, or it could be as complicated as consenting to adding new family members into the household. It also means that since they (at least at the age she's at now) lack any real concept or awareness of time and what time means, you will be pummeled with requests for an update on whatever thing you promised them approximately every thirty seconds. This also will not change whether or not it is three days or three weeks between whatever promise was made and its ultimate fulfillment.

This situation was, unsurprisingly, no different.

The second that yes left my mouth, it was immediately followed up by…yep, you guessed it. WHEN? When can we get fish, Mommy? Can we get them today? How many can we get? We should go right now. I think we should get A LOT of fish. Is the store open now? Which store do we go to? Can I look at the kitties while we're there? I want to pick out toys for my fish. If we got a kitty someday, would it eat the fish? I bet Daddy won't ever let us get a cat, though. But he likes dogs sometimes. Do you think a doggie would eat a fish?

Before we went near any pet store, I made sure to prepare her for the fact that we would have to set up the tank and wait a day or two before we could put fish in. I held her excitement at bay by assuring her we could get the plants and other decorative elements for it and put those in. I also established a firm expectation (or at least what I thought was firm) that she would have to do some of the work in getting it all set up. We'd always been pretty active and intentional with involving her in responsibilities at home, so I felt comfortable I could hold her attention during the process.

Perhaps "cocky" would have been a more appropriate word choice than comfortable, in retrospect.

The first stop at the pet store was of course the wall of adorable kittens and cats up for adoption. I'm not sure if she was reminding me or reminding herself, but she reiterated that Dad would NOT be letting us get a cat, even though the little black and white one was sooooooo cute. A few more oohs and ahhs and about seventeen more reminders from me not to tap on the glass, and we were off to the aquatic section.

I'm not sure what part of her personality this is, but I suspect it comes from my husband, who secretly loves to shop. She stopped on every single aisle to exclaim over the pet toys, look at the adorable collars, declare a dog bed the cutest thing she'd ever seen, and make sure I saw exactly how darling each and every one of the little pet outfits were. It made no difference to her that we had no other pets at home. The pet couture and accessories were still deeply appreciated by my fashion-conscious daughter. Approximately eleven hours later (five-year-old time moves differently for adults), we made it back to where the aquariums were. Exactly $186.08 later, our starter tank set, a bag of gravel—the neon pink, blue, and green kind, naturally—three plants, and one heart-shaped tank decoration officially made their entrance to the Team Lance abode. I reminded her of her commitment to help me set everything up when she tried to skip out on helping carry everything in.

Side note – this is one of the funniest, and sometimes, when I'm a tad more on the depleted side, infuriating things about her at this age right now. I am often doing the "mom carry," which involves trying to hold my purse, two bags of groceries, the old coffee cup from my cupholder, the keys, and her door open while she gets out of the car, and she will literally look at me and ask me to carry her or carry something inordinately tiny like her empty lemonade cup or a stuffy she absolutely had to bring with her on the fourteen-minute round trip errand we just ran. I realize empathy won't kick in for a few more years—fingers crossed—and she lacks the context to see anything other than herself, but seriously!?!

We settled into the kitchen, her with the job of unpacking everything from the bags and me suddenly realizing the full extent of what I'd gotten us into. Or, rather, what I'd gotten myself into. I'm not exactly mechanically minded or inclined for anything that requires following assembly and any sort of set-up directions. It's not totally out of the realm of possibility, but let's just say it's not my strong suit. About an hour and five minutes later, the gravel had been rinsed, and the decorative items were cleaned off and placed intentionally around the tank after a protracted conversation about why we might not want to bunch them all together in one place and leave the rest of the tank empty (not too dissimilar from our Christmas adventures of Em decorating the tree and bunching together all of the ornaments in one place instead of spreading them around).

We added water, and by "we" I definitely mean just me. By this point in the game, she was already up to her eyebrows in what sounded like a rousing game of pretending to be a veterinarian for her stuffies and doctor to the Barbies that needed help. I was simultaneously intrigued and a bit terrified that both could be treated at the same place, but I suppose when painter's tape is what all the casts and bandages are made out of, one must adjust their standards.

Another side note here—the painter's tape was a substitute for actual tape because I learned the hard way that if I left her unattended, that shit would end up not just on her Barbies and stuffies but all over my walls, my shoelaces, the doorknobs, and the back sliding glass door. I was less concerned about the amount of doll hair and fake fur I'd ripped out, but scraping tape off the glass of a door that got full sun for the majority of the day in the Arizona heat was not my idea of a good time.

Two days later, we were ready for some new fish friends! Emersyn had already fallen in love with the bright neon GloFish, so those were a given. She picked out a neon greenish-yellow one, a brilliant orange one, and a bright reddish-pink one that reminded me of the exact color of my favorite crayon when I was little. World, meet Maddie, Tuna, and…Darkness.

Cue the record scratch.

As she shared with me the names of her fish, I couldn't help but burst out laughing at "Darkness" as one of the names that she'd selected. Em hates to be laughed at, so I usually try to be very restrained when I laugh at something she's said so she doesn't misinterpret my reaction. This caught me so off guard, however, I couldn't help it. Her little brow furrowed, creating the most impossibly tiny and insanely adorable crease between her eyebrows. I could tell she was sizing me up and trying to see if I was being an asshole or not.

"I just wasn't expecting the name Darkness, honey. I love it! I swear I'm laughing with joy!" I tried to pour all of my enthusiasm and love for my little one into that statement, seeing that it was important to her. I must have passed the test because she went back to watching her new fishies. A few days later, Darkness morphed into being called Midnight instead. Still inappropriately dark and fairly hilarious, though! Eventually, the name got downgraded to just "Pinkie," and it's been that ever since.

We aren't entirely certain where "Tuna" came from, although perhaps it's just as simply self-evident as it could be. We did try to convince her to stick with this as a theme and name the pink one Spicy Tuna and the green one Avocado Roll so all of our favorite sushi orders would be represented, but she wasn't having any of that. Maddie, as a name, however, originated from the first time she met her kindergarten teacher. Prior to kindergarten, she used to teach dance, and there must have been a naming convention to use their first names, so she inadvertently introduced herself first as Miss Maddie instead. Em heard that, and for the next two weeks, all the stuffies and all the dolls were suddenly named Maddie, and she followed suit when naming her fish.

I must confess that I had been so focused on all of the set-up instructions and trying to make an inhabitable home for these creatures, I never even thought to ask about maintenance and cleaning the tank. I'm convinced I am working off what appears to be some early childhood karma of my own. I relayed this story to my dad later, and he laughed his ass off because, according to him, of course, I wouldn't know anything about maintaining a fish tank! We'd had one for quite a while when I was little, and although it was in my room and I can tell you what some of the fish looked like and how we used to bring home minnows from the lake to try and put them in the tank, I most certainly could not tell you what was ever done to that aquarium to keep it clean or maintained. Obviously, that chore had fallen to my poor parents because here I was in my forties, completely clueless about this.

I figured out by about day four or five that perhaps we should get one of those fish that liked to help with cleaning the tank, so back to the pet store we went, eager to adopt another new friend. As the store employee was attempting to scoop out the tiny black and white catfish, she almost netted one that appeared to be half-dead. I wasn't even sure she realized it at first, so I joked, "How about one that won't die on us immediately?" Famous last words.

We brought our new friend, Oreo, home and successfully integrated the new fish into the tank. The day went on and everyone seemed to be swimming around just fine. When it came time for bedtime, and it was time to turn off the tank lights, I realized little Oreo didn't seem like he was doing too well. Although I rarely agree with using hope as a method, that's exactly what I did that night, opting not to say anything to Em as I was unsure of her existing level of attachment to Oreo.

Sadly, Oreo didn't make it through the night. The morning check-in of the tank revealed the poor little scaly body of Oreo stuck up against the filter. I had to explain to Em that the new fish didn't make it, but we would try again. She was concerned but not too disappointed, and off to school we went.

The part of all of this that truly surprised me, however, was the enormous and inordinate amount of guilt I felt. In the years since we said goodbye to my dog, Nala, I seemed to have forgotten the depth of responsibility and empathy I feel toward any living thing in my care. I do not have a green thumb by any means, and I try to be cautious about what plants I become responsible for because even when I kill one of those, I feel horrible for days. In between my meetings and errands that day, I was swamped with feeling terrible for poor Oreo. Em had handled it like a champ this morning, and although she was sad, I think she was excited about getting a replacement fish.

When my husband came home and I whispered to him that I wanted to get Oreo 2.0, he offhandedly remarked, "Could you please bring home a healthy one this time? I don't think that little guy was good from the get-go." Well, shit. Per my usual pattern, it hadn't occurred to me that the death of Oreo could *possibly* be something other than my fault. Who knew these tiny little aquatic creatures could prompt so much personal growth?

Safely ensconced in her (or his) new home, Oreo 2.0 has settled in nicely and done an excellent job keeping the tank clean. By the time I'd had my revelation about the fact that, duh, yes, I need to do things to keep the tank clean, let's just say the water wasn't crystal clear, and I was noticing Maddie was starting to swim a little slower. "Dear God, please don't do this," I prayed as I started Googling how to clean a ten-gallon freshwater tank. Shit. There was a lot more involved in this than I'd ever realized. Perhaps my husband's relentless resistance to all things pet-related wasn't total bullshit after all.

We performed a partial water change, cleaned the gravel, added all the stuff you're supposed to add, tested the water, and made sure everyone was doing ok. It seemed like a success until we again checked the tank at bedtime, and it was pretty obvious that Maddie didn't have a high likelihood of making it through the night. Cue again my internal monologue assuring me that I was a horrible fish killer and shouldn't have been given the responsibility of adopting these poor little animals in the first place. I was certain Emersyn would take this hard. Before we turned the lights off for the night, I gently told Em that Maddie may not make it to the morning and seemed like she was dying.

Again, I was unsure of what to expect here. Maddie appeared to be the favorite, with her being the most commented on. Given the fact that this poor fish had been named after her beloved teacher, I supposed there could be a slightly different emotional connection than to, say, Darkness. Or Midnight. Or Pinkie. Whatever the fish's name was now.

Once again my child surprised me. She didn't miss a beat, put her little hands on her little hips, and said, "Well, Mom, if she dies overnight, we'll just have to unstick her from the filter, fish her out, and get a new one."

And you know what? She wasn't wrong.

I didn't bother to share all of this with her teacher, though.

A Thousand Dollars at Dairy Queen

I spent over a thousand dollars at Dairy Queen when I was pregnant.

In my defense, there was a store less than half a mile from my house. And it had a drive-through, for crying out loud. And did I mention I was pregnant? Now, before you get too far into judgment mode, let me remind you that a small Oreo blizzard (blended extra well, of course) runs close to $5.00. Add in a partner at home who prefers medium-sized blizzards and a stepdaughter who was there occasionally and was happy to get in on the DQ action, plus the duration of pregnancy, and… voilá. It actually doesn't take all that long to add up.

I estimated that, with an average weekly attendance of three times per week and average - extremely conservative estimate here—total cost of about $40/week for thirty-six weeks and expenses added up pretty quickly to $1,440.00. I would love to blame my husband and stepdaughter for the bulk of it, but I'm pretty sure even they got tired of the DQ dash toward the end of our adventure. I'm also pretty sure it explains the stretch marks…

Chalk it up to one more thing I've learned about myself since becoming a mom. But don't get me wrong—those blizzards definitely hit the spot.

Crying at School

In the months and weeks before Emersyn started kindergarten, people kept asking me how I was feeling about it. They wanted to know whether I was nervous or not. My kid had been going to someone else's house for daycare since she was four months old, and she'd been in a bona fide preschool since eighteen months of age. I'd mastered morning drop-off and after-school pickup. I'd figured out how to manage holidays when school was closed and even fall, winter, and spring breaks. We'd navigated gaps between summer sessions and found ways to adjust our schedules as needed to accommodate work, my husband coaching wrestling, and travel obligations.

But we'd never gone to kindergarten. Em's preschool was at a small, private Montessori. An environment where she knew all the staff, was familiar with the older kids, and where we said goodbye to the fish in the fish tank in the lobby every day before we headed to the car. It was a calm environment with lots of plants outside, a small garden onsite, and even a desert tortoise named Turtle-ini, arguably the best name for a desert tortoise ever. We loved the staff, and they did a great job with the kids.

The adventure of preschool with our kid, in particular, was her "leadership skills." This seemed to be the diplomatic way of referring to her control issues. Welcome to the club, Emersyn! Because it was a Montessori environment, it was very student-led, which was absolutely amazing for her independence. In our very first parent/teacher conference, her instructor shared they often referred to Em as the third teacher in the room. There was the head teacher, the assistant, and then Emersyn right there with them telling all the other kids what to do. I immediately had a crystal-clear picture in my head of her bossing everyone around with the absolutely and totally undeserved confidence of a preschooler. Truth be told, I was surreptitiously proud of this feedback.

As we moved into a new classroom, two of the additional critiques we kept hearing from her teacher were that she didn't choose any of the harder "works" (what they call the little workstations of activities in the room that the children self-select) and that when they participated in small group activities, Emersyn often coordinated it so she was directing the other kids in the group rather than doing the work herself.

It sounds like an exact 50/50 mix of me and Sean.

As we considered her learning style, our objectives as parents, her personality, the fact we happened to live in the highest-ranked school district in the state, and what we were hoping to get out of a school environment (oh yeah, and a private school tuition rate that cost more than our mortgage every month), we decided to enroll her in our nearby traditional public school. We took a tour and immediately fell in love with the principal. She had a big, bright personality, and Em and I both watched in awe as she navigated the hallways on giant platform heels. With my fashion-enamored daughter, it's entirely possible that's what closed the deal. Em was less interested in the academics and the amazing structures they had in place to support the kids through their educational journeys than she was in Principal DeGraffenreid's heels. I didn't care what it was that created the buy-in; I was happy my daughter was finally excited about this transition.

Despite the obviously enviable fashion choices of her soon-to-be principal, Em still tried to bargain with me, again channeling her inner Jimmy Hoffa to try and persuade me to make a change next year instead of this year. We eventually mutually agreed that it came down to a difference of opinion. Em felt we should switch next year (or never), and Sean and I felt the time was right to make a change. (Did I mention the private school tuition payment was more than our mortgage?)

The weeks went on, and we had all settled into the idea that Em would be starting a new school. Again, as the date drew closer, people continued to ask me how I was handling the change, wondering how I was doing. Full transparency here: I didn't get what all the fuss was about. It even struck me as a bit odd, maybe even a bit overblown. I mean, my kid had been going to school for a few years already, and I'd acclimated to that. This was a different building and a different routine to learn, but other than that, wasn't I already used to this?

No. No, I was not.

Fast forward to school supply shopping, and I was a hot mess. I cried when she picked out a backpack, snapped at my husband for not taking a million pictures of us checking off each individual item on the shopping list, and had a full-scale meltdown looking at baby photos of Em that night while Sean was putting her to bed. Em was predictably unruffled by my mom moments and barely tolerated the photos except as an excuse to perfect her picture poses. I always thought epic eye rolls would be reserved for middle school, but I can assure you she has already achieved expert level in this particular skill set.

Then came "Meet the Teacher" night, and I almost had an anxiety attack that afternoon because I simultaneously was so excited, emotional, and terrified I would forget all the things I needed to ask. In all truthfulness, I didn't *need* to ask anything. But tell that to my anxious mind when it's worked up. I dare you.

Sean originally wasn't going to be able to come because he was at a conference out of town, but he made the drive home just in time to join us. And yes, his willingness to make the extra effort made me cry, too. The school was amazing. It was welcoming and fun, and the entire place vibrated with a joyful sort of anticipation. Elementary school professionals are a unique and incredible gift to the world. We made it to her classroom to meet the now-famous Miss Lucky. Yes, her actual name. It felt like a little wink from the Universe that I could relax.

You know those cartoons where they get little hearts in their eyes that pop out when they see something they love? That's pretty much what it was like watching Emersyn meet Miss Lucky for the first time. Prior to this, Em was CERTAIN she would be assigned to the other kindergarten teacher. We had met him on our tour of the school, and his Spongebob SquarePants-themed aquarium had snagged her attention. Despite repeated efforts to tell her the final outcome might be different, she could not and would not be convinced otherwise. But did I even get to gloat about how right I had been? Oh, no, because Miss Lucky had entered the scene. The lovefest continued that evening because we also met Mr. Teddy.

Mr. Teddy was the amazing human in charge of the Kids Club before and after school. We enrolled Em in this so that we would have the freedom and flexibility to know she had somewhere safe to be in case we needed to go to work early, got stuck in traffic, or in case I was traveling. Em fell hard for Mr. Teddy—he made her laugh and feel welcome with his booming voice and huge smile. He won an everlasting place in Em's heart by displaying a significant and detailed interest in her day-to-day outfit choices. He always checked out her get-up and made sure he took note of the vibe and commented appropriately.

It wasn't uncommon for Emersyn to get dressed and ask me, "What do you think Mr. Teddy will think of this outfit, Mama?" Like the '80s Madonna vibe when Em discovered she could make her own leggings and fingerless gloves by cutting the feet out of her tights? Check. Unicorn dress, a pair of denim shorts, and a skirt (yes, under the dress) complete with pink cowgirl boots? Check. Sparkly gold tutu over a long skirt with a sequined tank top that had a sea turtle on it? Also check. Mr. Teddy knew how to boost her confidence and comfort in being her unique self.

We were so grateful he was there, not just because it made it easy to get her to go to school in the mornings and be ok with staying after for a bit, but because he genuinely cared about our child and the other kids in the program. You could tell by the way he interacted with them, greeted each of them, and commented on things that made them unique. It was quite a sight to behold, and we watched Em, over her first few weeks, absolutely blossom in a new environment that was so significantly different from the one she was in before.

My heart had been put so at ease through the first few weeks of meeting Miss Lucky, getting to know Mr. Teddy, and experiencing the force of nature that is Principal DeGraffenreid that I relaxed into it all. We were still having lots of firsts, and I knew we would still need to figure out school breaks and what happens when there is a little bump in the road, but I totally let my guard down. I felt absolutely comfortable about where we were. Perhaps I got a bit too satisfied with myself because the first time we went to curriculum night, and they had a "house party" for the kids, I was once again swept totally off of my emotional foundation.

I walked into a crowded gym. Kids were everywhere, parents were crammed along the walls, music was pumping in the background, a slide show was revolving on the giant screen at the front of the room, and as soon as the principal called it to order and invited the kids up, off my kiddo went.

Cue the tears.

Seriously, my eyes started leaking and my lip was quivering. I couldn't get my shit together. There was something so moving about watching my little one sit down next to a new friend and put her arm around her and be so at ease in this big environment that just a few weeks ago had seemed so overwhelming and intimidating. I saw firsthand how she was surrounded by people who loved working with and developing children. I witnessed the passion and exuberant joy of the educators and educational support teams who were creating this environment where my little one could grow. So yes, friends, I bawled. Hell, I'm tearing up now thinking of it.

This is one of those things nobody explains to you before you become a parent. Maybe there's not even a way to explain it. Maybe I wouldn't have listened or couldn't have understood. Maybe I'm perimenopausal, and it's not even that moving at all, just a function of my biology going a little haywire.

I kind of doubt that's what it is, though. Not that my biology isn't going haywire, because holy shit, that's its own journey for another book, but that my emotional state was due to that instead of the immense emotion of realizing I'm literally watching my child grow up in front of me.

I expected tears at school. I just didn't expect them to be mine.

After reading this one, I understand why all of my mom's friends and my extended family say Emersyn is exactly like me.

MORE NICKIE-ISMS   (KINDERGARTEN)

On Boys....

Nick: Mom, I got three more love notes today. But I threw two of them away. I told all three boys I was tired of getting these love notes.
MOM: Which one did you keep?
Nick: Oh, I kept Reed's. Reed's cute. He's not very smart, though.
MOM: Nick, I don't want these love notes going back and forth all the time when you're supposed to be doing class work.
Nick: I NEVER write love notes. I just get them. ALL the boys like me!
Mom: Oh, yeah? What sort of goofing around are you doing to get ALL the boys to like you?
Nick: I don't DO anything. They just think I'm cute.
Mom: Nickie, I think we need to talk about boys....
Nick: No, we don't need to talk. I already know everything about boys. Like how they act silly all the time and how they aren't as smart as girls.
Mom: Hmmmmm....maybe you do know enough...
Nick: Besides, Matthew dumped me yesterday so I don't have to worry about stupid love notes from him. He couldn't even spell my name right, anyway.

                         ****

On Bonamies....
Nick: Mom, what are those funny people, you know---bonamies?
Mom: What?
Nick: Bonamies! Bonamies! You know! I think it's a kind of people, like young people, maybe babies.
Mom: I haven't got the foggiest idea of what you're talking about.
Nick: Yes, you do! You know! I think it's also a kind of cat, too!
Mom: A kind of cat?? Nickie, I don't know what you're talking about
Nick: Yes, you DO know! I heard you say it one day! We even have two of them!!! WHAT ARE THEY???
Mom: Nicole! Calm down! Try to explain what you mean! What do they look like? Where are they, if we have two of them?

Nick: They're over by the fireplace---see? These bonamies!

Mom: SIAMESE! NOT BONAMIES! SIAMESE!!!

Nick: Gee, why are you yelling at me? All I did was ask...

****

On The Relative Value of Education

(Setting: a crowded Jack-In-the-Box at dinner time)

Nick: Mom, I can read now.

Mom: You can, huh? What can you read?

Nick: Oh, lots of things...you know. Like, that sign outside the window there. That reads "Jack-In-The-Box". See?

Mom: Very good, Nick...

Nick: And this little bag here: This reads "French Fries". And this paper cup reads "Iced Tea With Lemon".

Mom: HA! Gotcha! The words on that cup spell "cold drink" and the little bag says "fries". You were close, though.

Nick: Uh huh. I can read as good and even gooder than Ian. I have to go to the bathroom now. I can go all be myself and you don't have to take me at all. Know why?

Mom: Why?

Nick: Because I can read the letters on the doors now! I know which bathroom is for women and which one is for boys! (she gets up and dashes across the room)

Mom: Nickie! Wait!

Nick: (yelling) No, no, Mom! It's okay! I know which bathroom to use! I can read! I use the bathroom that says "Women"---it's the word that starts with the letter "M"!

****

On Security Factors...

Nick: Mom, Brett has a blankie, too, just like I do. But it smells REEEALY bad! It smells just their floor smells, and like their dog smells.

Mom: Well, 1 doubt that your blanket smells too great to Brett, either.

Nick: No way---MY blanket smells good. Do you promise I can keep

it until I'm a teenager?
Mom: Sure. You can keep it forever. You can even take it with you
when you get married and share it with your husband.
Nick: Not MY blanket. He'll have his own.
Mom: That's right, I forgot.
Nick: I'll just keep it and maybe when I have a baby I'll let him
use it! I hope he won't smell it up bad like Brett's. Did you know
Ian Alford still sucks his thumb? And he's in kindergarten!!
Mom: Some kids do that. It's not a big deal.
Nick: Yeah, but I know why he sucks his thumb. It's because he
doesn't have a blankie....not even a smelly one.

                              ****

On boys, II.
Nick: Mom, I told ALL the boys again that I was tired of getting
all these love notes and that they'd better stop. I was really
mad! I said, "No more!" But I told Reed and Matthew that they could
each write me just one more love note, but that is ALL!
Mom: Just one more, huh? That was nice of you...
Nick: That's right. I said one more each and it had to be a <u>good</u>
one, and then that's it!! No more!
Mom: What if they say "Take a hike, Nicole, we're not writing you
any more notes"?
Nick: Oh, ho! They'd NEVER do that!

This Cowboy Don't Need No Help

---◆●◆---

Emersyn is the only person on the planet who has gotten my husband to dance. Even at our wedding, he danced once with me, once with my mom, and once with one of his best friends, Travis.

Last night we went to a wedding. My cousin's son was getting married, and they had asked Em to be a flower girl. Emersyn immediately began counting down to this wedding. She'd only been to one wedding before, and she was so young she barely remembered that one except that there was dancing. I'm not sure she was quite certain what a flower girl was supposed to do or even what exactly weddings were all about, but she made sure she was going to be ready. With the amount of attention she'd suddenly been paying to songs with a heavy dance beat, and how frequently she was requesting to watch dance videos, it was clear she wasn't just prepping for a wedding. She was doing the dance equivalent of carb-loading for a marathon. She was planning a full-on takeover of the dance floor at the reception.

At the last wedding, her cousin, Grace, was her dancing partner. The two of them rocked that dance floor all night long, and we were all eagerly anticipating round two. I figured I'd be on the floor the majority of the time with her, but I was wrong. I was so wrong.

At first, Sean sort of did the obligatory twirl or two, but somewhere between Taylor Swift's "Love Story" and Abba's "Dancing Queen," my husband found his boogie shoes. And I don't mean just a cute sway or two here or there to a slow song; I mean full-on, sweat-through-his-shirt, hands-in-the-air, laugh-till-you-cry kind of dancing. I've never seen him do anything like this! I met his eyes on the dance floor, and the question was clearly written on my face. His eyes filled up with tears, and he gestured to Em and said, "It's this little girl. It's all her."

I guess my baby girl has some magic in her, even for her own dad, to unlock a new experience. They spent the next ninety minutes on the dance floor, spinning, jumping, and making pretty much everyone around them laugh hysterically. It made me cry with joy more than once.

Then, almost right at the hour and a half mark, Emersyn marched by, giving us the "come on, we're outta here" gesture, and just said, "Ok, I'm done. We're going." She didn't give two shits that I was in the middle of an epic singalong with my cousins, showing Em how it was really done, complete with my own amazing (ahem) dance moves. She was ready to go, so the party was over. There was no convincing her to stay. She barely tolerated us trying to sneak in a piece of cake before she barreled her way out the door toward the parking lot.

When she was not even quite two years old, her Uncle Brian started calling her Em the Gem, and it's a perfect fit. She has always had a giant personality. She's been a character pretty much from week one, flashing her famous smile early on. She's curious and into everything and loves attention. She even laughs with her whole body, just like I do. (She might have better dance moves, though.)

While all beings are multifaceted, it feels like Emersyn's facets both shine brighter and at the same time can show up darker. The moods are intense—big highs and big lows. I must admit this all feels acutely familiar.

From her first year, she's also had an intense desire for control of her situation, her decisions, her life. I can't say that I blame her! She'll have to learn to navigate compromise someday, but at the moment she marched off the dance floor, she was fully in charge of the situation and knew it. Hence, her comfort and self-assurance that it was time to leave the wedding reception. Obviously, this is an element of development for children as they assert their independence and figure out who they are in the world. Sean and I have tried to do our best to give her as much space as possible to be who she wants to be. (Without sacrificing wedding cake!)

One of the ways this has also manifested is through her clothes. Right around her two-year mark, I had big visions of cute, coordinated outfits with perfectly accessorized hair bows and headbands and matching Adidas sweatsuits for the whole family.

I couldn't have been more wrong.

The hair bows and headbands were never a thing. Even as a baby, we'd show up for outings or get-togethers with friends who had kids the same age, and while they completely ignored the cranial decorations my friends had placed on their noggins, my child would unceremoniously rip hers off and deposit them exactly where she thought they belonged: the floor.

Likewise, the cute little outfits and Adidas sweatsuits I'd painstakingly ordered went by the wayside. She wanted to layer, to mix and match, or to wear "mitch-match" as we call it. She started pairing bright green, rainbow and leprechaun-hat-covered St. Patrick's Day leggings with a sparkly pink sequined tutu, a blue shirt from her school, and neon-colored hand-me-down Vans from her cousin. Oh, and of course the socks can't match.

The other day for kindergarten she wore 'clip-clop' shoes (what she calls the shoes with the little heels on them) covered in blue sparkles and pictures of Ana and Elsa, turquoise green socks with corgis printed all over them, rainbow unicorn leggings, a black skirt covered in multicolored ribbons, and a hot pink shirt with orange daisies on it. Now, mind you, I've grown to love and embrace her style. It brings me joy to see the color combinations, and I have a fair amount of text threads with Em's Outfit of the Day photos.

It just wasn't what I expected.

Yet another of the things about becoming a mom that has surprised me is how much kids are already their own little person. Of course they're learning to assert their own boundaries as they grow, but I've been amazed at how determined Em already is in her opinions. This also includes opinions that are contrary to mine when it comes to getting ready in the morning, what we should or shouldn't have for dinner, and, well, pretty much everything else. In fact, she is currently on the floor behind me while I'm typing, asserting her opinion at an ear-splitting decibel level and throwing a fit because it's time to get ready for school, but she wants to paint her nails instead, and I've said no. I'm being educated on all the ways I say no to her and just how rude (one of her new favorite words to fling out when she gets upset) I am.

And then one of those facets of Em the Gem shifts just a bit, and the light catches a different part of her personality. She regulates and asks me to put buns in her hair, cracking up both of us when they come out looking more like Minnie Mouse ears than the cute little messy buns some of her friends wear. I watch her in the mirror, making duck lips and surprised faces at herself, a bit in awe of how in love with herself she is. What would it be like if I was that fascinated, appreciative, and enamored with my own self?

That's the thing about all those parenting adages and sayings. Things like, "Your children will be your greatest teacher." It's easy to yeah-yeah those things…until you have kids of your own that you're responsible for. Then you see it firsthand, and it's like, "Shit! People were right about this!" The humbling of the ego that comes either through realizations like this or through getting smacked in the face by something you never saw coming is immeasurable. Valuable, for sure, but the quantity of them is mindblowing.

One of my other favorite facets of Em the Gem is her general fearlessness. From the time she was teeny-tiny, she has been almost completely unafraid of the world around her. When she was about three years old, we were in Sedona with some of our beloved family members. Sean and her Uncle Brian were going to hike up a small part of the mountain behind us. The guys started heading up, and I thought Em would stay behind with my cousin, Ellen, and me. Maybe she'd play in the dirt a bit, have a snack, whatever. Oh no. Not Emersyn. My child was determined that if Dad and

Uncle Brian were going hiking, then dammit, so was she!

They'd already made it a ways down a path toward the base of the mountain when Em came charging right along behind them. In her sparkly pink cowboy boots, she was obviously well-equipped for climbing. Sure enough, she weaved her way in between the two men and took the lead heading up the hill. A ways up, she started to slip a bit on some of the dirt and loose rocks. When offered help, she looked right at her uncle and said, "This cowboy don't need no help," and proceeded to try and make her own way up. When I read this section to Sean after writing it, he informed me that she also peed off the rock at the top of the hill, just like the guys, too. I wasn't surprised.

Ah, to have a child who is exactly like me. It's both thrilling and terrifying! I remind myself often that this stubborn independence will absolutely be an asset to her along the way.

We've just got to get through the next thirteen years first.

5:00 a.m. Guilt Trips

"Mommy, you know what my favorite thing is? When you're home and being with you."

Even though it wasn't even 5:40 a.m., this is how my daughter started my day this morning. Well, to be totally truthful, she started it by stealth-walking like the world's tiniest ninja right up to the edge of the bed and then slamming two hands down about six inches from my face while whisper-shouting, "I'm awake!!!" The sun hadn't even started to rise yet, so I encouraged her to snuggle up next to me and desperately hoped to whatever parenting gods might exist that she would fall back asleep. She was quiet for a whopping thirty-seven seconds, although "quiet" is a completely relative term, as she was squirming around and making soft popping noises with her lips while jabbing her bony little knees right into the fleshy part of my thigh. I was just starting to relax again when she made that statement, "Mommy, you know what my favorite thing is? When you're home and being with you."

Hearing something like that before you're even fully back to regular states of consciousness will melt your mommy heart. I hugged her a bit closer and was starting to respond, "Aww, thanks, baby…" when she continued. "But my least favorite thing is when you go away, and you're not home. That makes me really sad."

Well, shit. Any hope of going back to sleep evaporated with that single statement. I had just been out of town for two nights on a work trip, and even though I made sure I was the one to take her to school the day I left and raced home to be there for bedtime the day I came back, it's clear that in the mind of my child, none of that erases the fact that I was gone for two nights. Ugh. Nothing like a heaping dose of guilt before the sun was up.

Childhood trauma noted and promptly forgotten, she quickly switched gears and launched into an interrogation about whether or not girls have as many muscles as boys. Apparently, this debate had come up as a hot topic of conversation at school, and Emmy had some questions. She doesn't like being told she can't do anything, so I could immediately see her inherent dislike of any line of conversation that had a flavor of "girls can't do it." I just wasn't expecting this conversation before I was even fully awake.

It was kind of a bummer to realize the conversations in the kindergarten classroom were already getting into the boys vs. girls dynamic. Somehow, I thought (and hoped) that wouldn't happen until later. Or at all. I wasn't sure what to say, partially because I was still half asleep, so I simply responded, "What do you think, baby?" I do appreciate that Em took it from a somewhat academic perspective despite the pre-dawn hour. She reasoned that everybody has muscles, it's just that some of them look different. We both agreed and that seemed to satisfy the conversational thread for the time being, which I was immensely grateful for as my brain wasn't up to fully-functioning speed yet.

She ricocheted into her next focus - whether or not she could watch TV, of course, which was of much higher importance than her absentee Mom or the musculoskeletal structures of boys and girls. She headed out to the couch, and I flopped back onto my pillow to take a few breaths while the guilt subsided, and I pondered the intricacies of helping Em navigate a world still too focused on traditional gender norms and patriarchal notions.

It just felt a little early for the 5:00 a.m. hour.

I Think I'll Stick With Cats...

It's Saturday morning. Emersyn is already onto her second outfit of the day, deciding her first combo of neon splatter-painted pants and a princess dress wasn't quite the right vibe. It might still be winter outside, but she's embracing her inner summer in a tank top, shorts, and knee-high fuzzy panda socks for good measure. She's flitting around the house, ordering around her stuffies, creating worlds where Barbies, My Little Pony, and some poor little dolls she keeps taking the heads off of coexist simply to serve her every whim.

She pauses in the living room, glancing up briefly. The TV is providing a droning backdrop for the morning while most of my husband's interest is consumed by whatever game he's playing on his phone as he completes his annoyingly slow wake-up for the day. I'm partially tuned in while glancing at my Kindle occasionally. Unprompted, Em announces to the room, "I want to get married." I try to remain nonplussed, mostly so I can see just how far down this rabbit hole we might end up going while Sean's head snapped up so fast from his phone I was worried he might hurt himself. (I mean, in your late forties, almost everything is a risk!)

"Why, baby? What would be fun about marriage?" I inquired. "Because I want to get pregnant. And get a cat. I'll probably marry Nash. I don't know what he'll look like, though. He'll probably have a mustache like you, Dad. Then I can move out of this house and get my own house."

I tried my hardest to navigate the conversational whiplash occurring because of this exchange. I started by asking about having a baby and what she thought would be fun about it. As I delved a little further into expectations of motherhood like dirty diapers, crying babies, having to feed and clean up after them, Em wrinkled her little nose and scrunched up her face and said, "Well, I thought it would be fun. But that's a lot of work. Maybe we'll just adopt. Or maybe I'll just stick with cats…"

I didn't even get to explore the comment about why her future partner was likely to have a mustache like her dad because, with zero further comment, she zipped off to the next thing that caught her interest while Sean and I simply stared at each other for a few moments.

Fast forward a few months, and Em caught me off guard again on the way home from school. Now, mind you that we only live about a two-minute drive from the school, so it's not like there was an extensive amount of time to get into this conversation. I was barely pulling out of the school parking lot when her little voice piped up from the backseat, "Mom, when am I allowed to date?" I bobbled the iced tea I was just bringing to my lips and thought fast. I didn't want to get into too many details, so I relied on one of my favorite go-to tactics with her: less is more. "Eighteen," I replied, with no additional information.

I glanced in the rearview mirror as I came to a stop in the right-hand turn lane and watched her tiny brow furrow as she mentally tried to calculate how far in the future that might be. She must have decided it wasn't worth the effort because she just responded, "Shoot."

Thinking I was off the hook, I inwardly gave myself an atta-mom and a mental pat on the back and took a sip of my tea when she followed up her question immediately with, "Well, when can I get my lip pierced?" I barely choked down the liquid threatening to come back out of my nose. "Also eighteen," was the response. My brain activated into overdrive with various images of a high-school-aged Emersyn in her rebellious phase. Sean and I already agreed that we'll be supportive of how Em wants to present herself to the world, but that was a rabbit hole I slid down FAST. I pulled into the driveway, pretty confident we were done with the conversation when she met my eyes in the rearview mirror. "What about my nose?"

"Seventeen with good behavior," flew out of my mouth as I tried to process the conversation we were having. "Em, where is this coming from?" I asked.

"Well, Auntie Ellen has one. And so does Miss Kristyn. So I just thought I could get one, too."

For context, her Auntie Ellen does have her nose pierced, and so does Miss Kristyn, the bride who Emmy was a flower girl for in a wedding about five months prior to this conversation. I was amazed at Em's thread of logic, however. She hadn't even seen Auntie Ellen or Miss Kristyn in months. She wasn't happy with just getting eighteen years old as her answer, so I appreciate her consideration that perhaps if she brought in additional evidence for other requests with more context, I might be supportive. It's not a bad line of reasoning. "Seventeen with good behavior," I repeated. "How about a popsicle?" And with that, we were off for more after-school adventures and no more discussion of body piercings of any kind.

This girl is already a force to be reckoned with, and I don't anticipate that lessening over the years. It's still too soon to be picking out jewelry, but it also might not be as far away as we were hoping, either!

Mothering Without a Mother

———◆•◆———

I lost my mom when I was thirty-one years old. Unexpected, totally out of the blue. A complete shock. I'm writing this eleven years later, and it still hurts like hell.

Since I'd never planned on having children of my own in addition to my bonus stepdaughter, it didn't cross my mind that this was a journey that would also shift once I had a child. Fast forward years later to my unexpected (aka "HOLY SHIT!") pregnancy, and I realized quickly that I was missing out on something that would have been an integral part of my picture.

I was one of those fortunate ones who had the extreme privilege of having not just a great mom but an *amazing* mom. I legitimately counted her as one of my best friends, and she was one of my first phone calls whenever anything excellent, challenging, or even just plain old ordinary happened. Even a decade later, I occasionally still reach for my phone to give her a ring or shoot her a text.

The morning I had the first positive pregnancy test result, my initial freakout was immediately compounded by a wave of grief so severe I ended up on the floor, slumped against the side of the couch. (Not sure why I couldn't have landed ON the couch, but the floor seemed to be the right space for some reason.) I bawled for my mom, for all my fears and what-ifs and what-might-not-be's, and because I wanted to call my momma, dammit. Yes, I still had my dad to call, and eventually did. Yes, I had other friends I could call, and eventually did. And yes, I wanted my mom with me.

I'm a pretty spiritual person, and I feel connected with my mom still even though she's transitioned to whatever the heck happens after we die. She shows up in some very interesting ways or I get reminders of her when I'm not expecting it. Sometimes I'll hear from a friend of hers occasionally and it helps me feel a little bit of that love. But it's not the same.

There wasn't anyone to call throughout my pregnancy to ask questions about what her pregnancies were like. Did she have high blood pressure? Was she prone to back labor? Did her feet swell into puffy little loaves of bread-like-looking things like mine were? Why did she have two C-sections? Was there something I should let my doctors know? Was it normal to be this terrified about becoming a mother? And what about my baby shower? Mom would have been beyond thrilled to put together a baby shower. She went above and beyond for my bridal shower, and I can only imagine what it would have been like for her to have gotten to celebrate another grandbaby in the family. She died before my niece was born, so she never got to meet her, but she did throw a lovely baby shower for my sister-in-law, and I can still remember how she practically vibrated with excitement over doing it.

Pregnancy hormones are no joke, and after almost twenty-four hours of labor, preeclampsia, multiple rounds of seizure-inducing blood pressure levels followed by frightening drops in my heart rate and loss of the baby's heart rate, I was wheeled in for an emergency Cesarean section. I warned the anesthesiologist I didn't respond well to anesthesia and usually required some extra attention.

Sure enough, whether it was minutes or decades later, I could feel the nurse's knuckles pressing into my open incision as they sewed me up, and I looked up in panic at the doctors. The anesthesiologist quickly administered more, which had the side effect of making me feel like I was going to throw up. He gave me something to combat the nausea, and all I remember from that point on is a very blurry image of a doctor holding up my baby, I think I asked if she was healthy right before I passed out. The next four and a half hours exist only in bits and pieces, vague resurfacings from the drug cocktails my poor body had been ingesting for the past day and a half. I remember desperately wanting to wake up but knowing there was no way I could fight the pull of whatever narcotic was dragging me back into unconsciousness.

My poor husband sat in a room with the baby by himself for hours, not knowing what was going on with me. That might be the part I'm most upset about. I can't imagine what might have been going through his head. Afterwards, I felt robbed of those precious moments you always see in photos of mothers holding fuzzy-headed, squishy little newborns to their chests right after birth. My little one had to wait for hours to be in my arms, and even though I was unconscious for most of it, I felt robbed, too.

There was no one to call to share this story with right away who would understand it at the level I knew my mother intuitively would. Even though for the first time in my life I had a being who would supposedly and hopefully be with me until the end no matter what, I felt more alone than I ever had before.

I yearned for her then, and I still do. Sometimes, this feeling sweeps over me when I want to ask her what it was like to raise me and my brother. What struggles did she have? What was my little personality like? Did she miss her sleep as much as I do? Did she worry as much about everything as I do? Did she constantly second-guess her mothering and feel simultaneously grateful/annoyed/guilty/overwhelmed like I do? How did she balance work and parenting? How did she balance work and parenting and marriage? Did she miss her unfettered independence sometimes? Did she crave more downtime with us? Did she get tired of never resting?

Sometimes being a mom myself triggers a deep wanting for my own mom, and not always in the halcyon glow of bittersweet longing. A wave of grief strikes. Not a quick little pang of missing her, but a legitimate, threaten-to-overtake-you tsunami of grief. It's hard when this happens because my first instinct is to numb it. Quell it in some way. Distract myself. Tone down those feelings. And yet, I also know that the sooner I feel them, the sooner it will round out at the edges, losing some sharpness. Occasionally it will usher in some sweetness, but not always. Sometimes, it's like I'm opening the lid off something carbonated, letting some of that pressure and fizz bubble out and over the edges. It doesn't lessen the liquid inside, but some of that tension is eased.

The intersection of grief and joy is real. And real hard. Some of the times I miss my mom the most aren't just when I need advice or a supportive ear as I whisper, "What the actual fuck?" It's not even always the times that are the best times, the sort of mountaintop moments. Often it's the most normal times, like playing cards with Sean and my dad now that Emersyn has finally learned to play Go Fish or Uno.

We grew up playing cards in my house. Euchre was the main game. Emmy doesn't get all the rules of it yet, but she loves sitting with all of us playing cards. There was a moment last night when I missed my mom so bad my teeth hurt. We were sitting on the patio out back of my dad's condo in the White Mountains in Arizona, having escaped the heat of Phoenix for the weekend. We dealt the first hand of Go Fish, and I realized it was the first time we'd all been able to sit around and play cards like this, the way I'd done so many nights growing up and so many nights as an adult with my family.

It's not that it robs me of my ability to be present in the moment. I've found a duality in which I can exist where I am fully present and joyfully engaged and still be wholly missing her at the same time. How would she be interacting with Emersyn? Would we still be partners for Euchre? Would she still be cussing out my husband when he beats her at a round of cards? (Most definitely.) In those moments, I'm keenly aware that I'm missing out on the partnering and co-mothering that would have been available if she was still here.

I snuggle my baby a little closer. I ask Sean for an extra hug. I text a friend. I tell my dad how much I love him. I call my brother. I write Mom a letter in my journal. I'll peek at her Facebook page just one more time. None of it is a substitute, but it gets me through.

Most importantly, it inspires me to show up for my own daughter even more.

Apparently storytelling has always been of interest to me…

Conversations with Nickie
Part I.

Nick: Mom, want to hear the good news and the bad news?
Mom: Sure, Nick, go ahead and tell me the good news.
Nick: Hmm. Think I'll start with the bad news. It was a stormy, stormy night. It was really raining outside...
Mom: Was there also lightning? And thunder?
Nick: Oh, yes. There was lots of lightnings and lots of funder.
Mom: You mean thunder.
Nick: Yeah, funder. And it was really, really raining outside.
Mom: So what happened?
Nick: The bad news is that there was a mom and a dad and a brother and they had no food to eat. The sister had food, though.
Mom: And?
Nick: There was also wolfs. And while they were looking for food, coyotes were coming over the fence to get them. Not the sister, though.
Mom: What's the good news?
Nick: They went to the store, Safeway, I think...Oh yes, and they all got food.
Mom: What about the wolves and the coyotes?
Nick: They ate each other.
Mom: Is that it? The whole story?
Nick: Yes. Also the bad news is that they lived in a little, tiny, tiny, tiny house. It was so tiny no wolfs or coyotes could ever get in.
Mom: Just like our house, right?
Nick: Right. Can we eat now?

Sex Scenes at the Car Wash

———◆•◆———

Reading trashy romance novels is one thing. Writing them is a whole other adventure.

I once joined a group where we committed to fifteen minutes per day for eighty-four days in a row, working on a creative project. I've always had a thing for what I lovingly refer to as "trashy romance novels," and I was particularly intrigued to try and write one. My mom would have laughingly referred to these types of books as "bodice rippers." When the project kicked off, I was excited to use the time try my hand at some steamy scenes.

The only slight problem with this was that it was summertime, so school schedules were a bit weird, we were traveling a lot, and I didn't have the regularity that the school year brings. This wasn't a bad thing; it just meant that I was staying up later than usual, sleeping a bit later than usual, and my daughter was home more. Even with my earbuds in and with a white noise soundtrack blaring, I quickly learned that I can't write much in the way of romance while sitting on the couch with my daughter with *Bubble Guppies* blaring on the TV. There was something about time and place that was important.

This meant I had to get more intentional about making time to write, and it also meant I had to lean on my ingenuity to get it to happen. I joke about how kids will suck you dry and take all of your time, and it's not for nothing! It is almost without fail that the second I start to get immersed in some task, my daughter, who up until that point could literally give two shits whether or not I'm in the house, suddenly senses my shift in focus, and I become the most interesting and critical focal point in the household.

So, as I was pursuing this eighty-four-day project and finding that I needed solo space where I was undisturbed, I found myself sitting at the car wash one morning, writing a sex scene. Kind of like a coffee shop, the ambient noise and hustling of the car wash created that sort of background noise effect that seems to help me find a creative space. Unlike a coffee shop, where sometimes I can pick up the energy of the people around me, or I might get worried that someone walking by will glance at my laptop and see the word S-E-X (or something more descriptive!), the car wash created an oddly conducive environment for me to write.

Before I had Em, if you had told me that one of the adventures becoming a mother would bring me would be me writing trashy romance novels at a car wash, I wouldn't have believed you.

This journey sure as hell has a lot of surprises.

Howling at the Ocean

Watching Em at the beach is perhaps the single most joyful thing I've ever witnessed.

She goes full out. No holds barred, barely stops for breath. Her little legs are pumping the entire time, running into the surf, running back on the sand, running to see the shell I found for her, running back over to where she's digging. Running, running, running, and it's all so damn joyful. She howls at the waves, screams at the water, "Come get me, ocean!" and then shrieks in delight and fake alarm as she gets splashed mercilessly.

It feels like the ocean is laughing with her.

Maybe she is in on some kind of cosmic joke I'm not privy to. It certainly seems that way. Her connection with the sand and the water and even the sun seem complete. Fused together, even. Her hair curls tighter, and her eyes shine brighter. She is every bit who I want to be—maybe who I am deep down in my core—when she's at the ocean.

I envy the carefree experience she has. I'm jealous of the total relaxation and full presence. As I'm searching for riptides, large swells, perhaps an errant jellyfish or—god, is that a shark fin or a dolphin?—she simply is. She is fully present with every fiber of her being in the moment. It's like she relaxes into knowing the Universe has her back and is right there with her, laughing and shrieking right alongside her. She's everything light and good and beautiful, all in a moment.

I want to play like that. Not even at the beach, but in my daily life. Fully present, completely free from the fears of what could be and what might be and what may possibly happen. I bet my shoulders would relax more.

I'd probably sleep better, too. I'm not judging myself here; just building an awareness.

This child came to teach me, not the other way around.

I can't imagine having TWO of Emersyn running around.

Conversations With Ian
--a discussion in non-sexist behavior.

Scene 1: Nickie is shrieking in dramatic agony (no tears apparent)
and screams in my face: Ian hit me! In the <u>stomach</u>!
Mom: Ian, come in here immediately!
Ian: Just a minute...I have to put away my dinosaurs and clean up my
room and finish looking at this book.
Mom: IAN!!
Nickie: IAN! MOM WANTS YOU HERE TO BEAT YOU! COME NOW!
Ian: I didn't really hit her in the stomach. It was more like her
bumper.
Mom: Her what?
Ian: You know. Her behind.
Nickie: No! No! It was my stomach! My stomach! And it will still
hurt tomorrow day!!
Mom: Ian, you know you're not ever supposed to hit girls in the
stomach. I've told you that before. Don't you remember?
Ian: Yeah. But you can really get boys in the stomach, huh?
Mom: No, you shouldn't be hitting anybody anywhere, but you especially
shouldn't hit girls in the stomach.
Nickie: Mom, will you spank him if he hit me in the head? He did!
He hit me in the head!
Ian: Yeah, I remember. Girls might have babies in there so you
shouldn't hit them because you might hurt the babies.
Mom: Well, that's close. It's more like girls' stomachs might be
able to grow babies some day but if they get hit too much they won't
be able to have babies if they want them.
Nickie: Can I have a baby in my belly? Please? A brown Cabbage
Patch baby. Please?
Ian: Ha! Did you hear what Nickie said, Mom? A baby in her belly!
Mom: Some day Nickie could have a baby, Ian.
Nickie: See Ian? I told you so!! But you can't have one, you can't
have one!!
Ian: Can I go play with my dinosaurs now?
Mom: I take it we're all done with talking about babies and bellies.

Ian: Yeah. There's nothing else to say about it. I won't hit girls' babies in the belly. I mean girls' stomachs.
Mom: Good. Don't be hitting anybody any time, okay?

Scene 2: Five minutes later:
Mom: Ian! Why is Nickie screaming again??
Ian: She hit me and I hit her back.
Mom: I thought we had all this hitting straightened out. What happened?
Nickie: Ian hit me! Ian hit me! Again!
Ian: You hit me first!
Nickie: Boys are rotten! Boys are stupid!
Mom: Stop it-I can't stand this yelling. Why are you two fighting so much?
Ian: Because Nickie won't leave me alone and I want to play by myself.
Nickie: No, Ian! Don't leave me alone! You're my friend! I won't hit you any more!
Mom: Can't you please get along for just a few minutes?
Ian: Well, okay, Mom. But just for a few minutes.
Mom: Thanks, Ian. You're a pal.
Nickie: See, Ian? Mom likes you again! Now can I be Frank Hardy?
Ian: Okay. I'll be Joe. Mom, you have to be Mr. Hardy. Tell Frank and Joe to go off by themselves outside and hunt for clues.
Mom: Gee, do I have to? Well, okay...Bye Frank and Joe. Have fun hunting for clues!

Jiu-Jitsu Dads

Dads are an interesting species.

Before I had my own daughter, there was a very confident part of me who genuinely thought I understood this genre of human beings, but it turns out there were two kinds of dads I'd never encountered before: jiu-jitsu dads and trampoline park dads.

My first foray into the world of Brazilian Jiu-Jitsu came because my four-year-old daughter had expressed interest in trying it. Of course, for my husband, this fulfilled every childhood dream of his own, and we (both admittedly and immediately) got swept up in the excitement of cool shirts, branded water bottles, and getting our daughter her first gi. Of course she chose the bright pink one, and we had a bit of a hard time when we had to tell her she wasn't allowed to also have a perfectly accessorized bright pink belt but instead needed to wear the standard-issue white one that all beginners wore. Perhaps that should have been my first clue about her projected longevity with the art. There was an amazing gym near our house with two of the most incredible human beings leading it. In addition to the classes offered throughout the week, Saturdays were parent/child classes from 9:00–10:00 a.m.

When I first signed up my daughter for classes in January, it never once crossed my mind to think more deeply about the schedule beyond "Sure, I can get her there on time once or twice a week." This was a passion and interest of my husband's, so clearly he would be the one taking the lead with everything, even if I was the one to take her during the week since his work schedule wasn't conducive to that from a timing standpoint. I hadn't quite taken into consideration the fact that my husband was neck-deep in coaching girls' wrestling, and the season extends well into the end of February. It seemed pretty manageable for that first week, even if my daughter bawled her way through her first class, and the emotional load was a bit more than I was originally prepared to navigate.

The real error of my ways made itself apparent when I figured out that there would be seven Saturdays where I was going to be the parent in the "parent/child class" combo. Ok, cool, I'd consider it a bonding opportunity, maybe a light workout…. No big deal, right?

Until I met the jiu-jitsu dads.

There were about thirteen kid/parent combos the first Saturday I went. It hadn't occurred to me that I might be the only mom in the group until I took a look around the gym and noticed that was the case. My intimidation factor rose a few percentage points, but I was there for my kid, not for all these other people, so it wasn't that big of a deal. Truthfully, it made me a bit prouder to show all the kids in the class that moms could do this, too. I saw a few beer bellies here and there—on the dads, not the kids—and figured I could hang, at least with that group. There were also five dads that showed up in gis of their own, obviously guys who practiced jiu-jitsu themselves. I immediately named them "the jiu-jitsu dads" in my head. One bowed and stepped onto the mat with his daughter, who was about seven years old. He went straight for her ankles and tackled her, then popped up, grinning and barking at her to get up.

For her sake, she seemed really into it and was grinning, too, so it didn't raise any red flags, but his intensity was like a blast across the room. Then you had the other dad whose kid I recognized from class as one of the ones who was pretty exceptional for his age and was frequently called on to demonstrate. Based on how his dad was stretching and strutting, it looked like Saturday morning classes would be his turn to outshine his son. There was a focused intention that seemed to broadcast, "I'm not here for fun!" The other jiu-jitsu dads were slightly dialed-down versions of this but similar in stance, alertness, and focus, oozing competitiveness. They left me with the impression they were each just hoping something happened that would allow them to fight for real. It was a bit much for my taste.

Class started, and when I began to breathe heavily three minutes into the warm-up, I realized I might have bitten off more than I could chew. I wasn't in terrible shape, but I wasn't winning any bodybuilding awards anytime soon, either. As part of the warm-up, they had us line up on the side of the mats with our kids, and in groups of five pairs, we would run, frog leap, and bear crawl all the way across the mats. Minus the throbbing in the knee I had reconstructed a few years back, this was all pretty fun with plenty of giggles in between the mini-sprint races. Until we got to the "bear crawl with your kid on your back" round.

"What the actual fuck?" I panted under my breath. They wanted me to get down on my hands and knees, hoist my very wiggly, very unwieldy, not-very-coordinated four-year-old onto my back somehow, then expect her to hang on while I crawled like a bear across the mats, which suddenly seemed about a mile wide. I was about halfway back through the line, so I got to observe the first sets of parents and kiddos. It became abundantly clear that all of them had done this before—they looked like Formula 1 race car pit crews, getting into place with a practiced precision and crystal clear understanding of their roles. The jiu-jitsu dads made up the majority of the first two groups to go, and I watched them hustle over to their spaces and throw themselves down while the kids popped up effortlessly onto their backs. This was followed by viciously whispered orders for the kids to lock their arms and get their grips. We were obviously moving into the competition mode of the warm-up.

When it was time for me and Emersyn to go, we were much less fully coordinated, smoothly-executing Formula 1 racing team and more "toddler on tricycle." We couldn't quite figure out the right way for her to hang on, so when I attempted to move forward so we weren't still on the starting line when all the other teams were already done, she slid right off my back and pulled both of us onto the floor. I finally opted to make it funny and tickled her until she let go so we could just run across the mat instead. I lined up, looking for a fellow parent to laugh with, but met the eyes of no one. Whether they were averting their eyes to be polite and save me from my own embarrassment or because they were afraid I would try and associate with them is still unclear to me. I was on my own.

Class progressed, and we eventually made it to the sparring part of the ordeal. This was a time for the parents to do some free sparring with their kids, allegedly to practice what we'd been learning as far as techniques go. Keep in mind that none of the kids in the class were over the age of seven, so you can imagine what this was like. For me and Em, it was more about tickling and giggling and me trying to get her to focus and try what we learned instead of staring at all the other kids in the class.

But for the jiu-jitsu dads…their moments had collectively arrived.

The air surrounding those pairs seemed to transform into something reminiscent of a one-sided UFC fight. I don't think the kids realized it, but the dads sure did. What had been a lighter, more playful vibe was now filled with intense instructions, sweat, and kids who weren't quite sure if they were having a fun time or not.

I survived more than my fair share of weekend classes with my kid before the "I want to try jiu-jitsu" vibe wore off for good. I thought I had unlocked a new level of motherhood achievement by my new in-depth understanding of the jiu-jitsu dad phenomenon. That lasted for a few months until I took my daughter to the indoor trampoline park and encountered trampoline park dads.

On the final day of her last year of pre-k, my daughter's school closed at 11:30 a.m. Always excited about an early pick-up, the night before she had asked me if we could do "whatever she wanted" after I picked her up from school. I try to do the "Yes Mom" thing as much as I can, and I had a pretty good idea of the still fairly limited scope of what she might ask to do. I felt good about the options, so I decided to indulge it. It was Pajama Day (a.k.a. The Best Day Ever), so when I picked her up she was still wearing her Moana nightgown. As I buckled her in her booster seat, she leaned right into my face and asked excitedly, "Can we go to the jumpy place?"

That's what she called the indoor trampoline park near our house. There were trampolines all over, a giant ball pit with things to climb and swing from, foam pits to jump into, and more germs than the human brain could possibly comprehend. I didn't care for the environment as it was loud, bright, and just big enough that it was hard to keep track of where she was, but she absolutely loved this place. We didn't go very often, but every once in a while, we'd say yes. Truthfully, I think the slushie machine might have played an equally important role in the attraction of the place as the trampolines did. Given that it was already over one hundred degrees in Phoenix and this place was a well-air-conditioned way to get her some good physical activity and put me in a place with decent Wi-Fi, I said yes.

As her hot pink, charm-covered Crocs led the way into the place, I noticed the family in front of us. It was a dad (or uncle, stepdad, father-figure type possibly, but I'm assuming dad because of the physical similarities) and his two kids. The boy looked to be around nine or ten, and the girl was maybe seven or eight years old. The first thing that caught my attention was the dad's posture and manner of walking. He wasn't just walking into this place; he was *strutting*. There was some serious man-swagger going on here. The second thing I noticed was they were already sporting their matching hot pink, electric blue, and neon yellow trademark trampoline park socks. In order to bounce here, you had to have an official pair of these socks. This particular pair they were sporting was the OG edition of the socks, which meant this family wasn't new to the trampoline park. These were monthly membership club types who knew a thing or two about a thing or two around this place.

The third thing that caught my eye was the way the dad was casing the place. He was sizing up the joint, scanning the various jumping areas, almost like he was plotting an attack. That was the moment I realized he wasn't truly there for his kids. I mean, sure, they happened to be along for the ride, but this was about him. Now, don't get me wrong—when a parent or caregiver can come to an experience and enjoy it equally as much as the kids (see: me at any aquarium or beach ever)—that's solid gold. But every once in a while, you encounter a parent who is having more fun than the kids, and that always creates an interesting experience.

I paid an exorbitant price for my daughter to gain access to the various trampolines, and we made our way over to an area where we could stow her shoes, and I could park it for a bit while she went off to bounce. It didn't take me long to locate that dad again. He was the one racing ahead of his kids to the giant run of trampolines where you could bounce from one to another if you were big enough, slam into a wall of trampolines, and then bounce your way back. Unfairly, perhaps, but I was imagining what was going through his head, guessing he was seeing himself in a slow-motion reel worthy of Red Bull TV, jumping gracefully from one springy section to the other.

I focused on my daughter and answered some emails on my phone until I found myself wandering over to the foam block pit part of the place where Em was gleefully launching herself off the edge like she was cannonballing into the pool. Emersyn was only five at the time, and she was still fairly little compared to the majority of the kids and people in the place, so I stayed close.

This was also the part of the park that had the "Pro Zone" trampolines. These are trampolines that bounce jumpers ultra high—higher than the other ones elsewhere in the building. There were two sections of trampoline with a lightly padded area between them, and the section was surrounded by see-through netting on two sides and padded siding that went about eight feet up the walls on the other two sides. TP Dad (as I called him in my head - TP for Trampoline Park) was perched on top of one of these walls, eyeing the trampoline below. His kids bounced lightly nearby, all attention on him. I could see the flush on his cheeks and the light sheen of sweat covering his forehead and tear-dropping down his temple. He was plotting again, no doubt picturing in his mind exactly how rad he was going to look with this bounce.

I wasn't quite sure if he had joined me in the over-forty crowd, but I could comfortably estimate the guy was at least in his mid-thirties. One of the things I learned quickly as I coasted into the middle of my thirties and over into the new decade was that the body does not repair itself as quickly as it used to. Also, things that might not have ever been painful or problematic before suddenly had a tendency to usher in aches and pains the likes of which you'd never seen before. As I watched him contemplate not IF he should jump but HOW, all I could think was, "His poor knees!"

Making sure he had his kids' full attention, he launched himself from the top of the wall into the center of the trampoline. However, instead of a giant bounce, it seemed as if the entire trampoline caved in on itself, and I heard a giant THWACK! He bounced up for sure, but it was clear the trampoline hadn't loved the weight or possibly the initial height from which he had jumped. I also noticed the telltale "ouch, that hurt my back" posture as he immediately walked out of the Pro Zone area. I imagined he was telling his kids that he "Just wasn't interested in jumping anymore." I kept an eye out for him over the next half hour or so, and although he still jumped with his kids, that early exuberance was gone, and he was holding that low back a little gingerly as they walked (not racing anymore) between the areas of the park.

I'd never been more appreciative of my lack of desire to behave like that in my entire life. Cheers to parenting without the compulsive need to recreate parts of my childhood that could possibly cause severe injuries. I'll stick with my dino-shaped chicken nuggets, thank you very much.

The Road Trip "Mom Con"

You've probably heard some variation of the saying, "If you travel with your kids, it's a trip. If you travel without your kids, that's a vacation." Boy, oh boy, is this one true.

First, there's the insane amount of shit you have to pack for these tiny little humans. In my experience, every trip with kids seems to require a ridiculous volume of items, pretty much in exactly the opposite proportion to the size of the child. The smaller they are, the more crap you have to cram in your vehicle, suitcase, or that impossibly tiny space underneath the seat in front of you on the plane.

Older kids need a phone and some earbuds. But little ones? They need eighty-seven daily outfit changes and sixty-three toys they probably won't want to play with, so you'll end up buying something new for them anyway: a travel high chair, bibs, bottles, and two different types of mineral-free, organic, ocean-safe sunscreen. You also need to bring a full box of new crayons that they will also not want to play with, so you'll end up giving them the pen that has been at the bottom of your purse for eons and is partially encrusted with tiny unchewed gum pieces, melted Chapstick, and heaven-only-knows-what-that-brown-thing-is.

Lastly, you must bring half your pantry in the form of snacks that you can only hope they will actually eat so you can stave off the hunger-related meltdown. It's ridiculous. And the worst part is that regardless of what you pack, there will inevitably be one significant item that, for whatever reason, you forgot. It's always too much, and yet it's never enough.

The lesson I keep learning the hard way, though, is what I call the "Mom Con" of packing a cooler and snacks, only for my daughter to go on a sudden and fierce hunger strike and refuse to eat anything except the meat out of a Lunchable and a single Capri Sun for all eight hours of travel.

The great thing about Em is that, unlike a lot of kids who will cheer wildly for a chance at a Happy Meal, she won't eat fast food. Like, any of it. Not tater tots from Sonic, no golden McDonald's fries, hell, I can't even talk her into a cheesy roll-up from Taco Bell. It's not a terrible thing! Don't get me wrong, I'm glad she's not into these things, and in the long run, it will either change or it will be a sustained positive approach around food.

The problem is it's a giant pain in the ass when we're traveling now.

I can't exactly stop and make her something when we're out on a back road somewhere, so we end up stocking a huge cooler. We'll bring fresh fruit, two different kinds of cheese, Goldfish crackers (because maybe this is the week where she's back to eating them), pretzels, dried mangos, fruit snacks, and anything else she's ever at any point eaten and liked so we have some semblance of hope of keeping her tummy full. Why is this such a big deal? Because when Em hasn't eaten, she doesn't just get hangry; she turns into a volcanic Godzilla erupting all over everyone and anything around her.

The Mom Con comes in when, despite all of this prep work, she decides to eat three strawberries, four pretzels, and a handful of blueberries for the entirety of the travel day. One of the times we went to visit my brother and his family, Em pulled this approach despite our customized cooler buffet. When we got to their house, she was too busy playing to eat, so by the time we made it back to the hotel and negotiated a quick shower, we were entering Godzilla territory. Combine that with a kid who generally hates going to bed on a good day, and we were primed for failure. At this point, she plowed through a string cheese, wanted some strawberries, and tore up her favorite snack: blueberries. Sean and I were both glad she finally had a full belly and hoped it would let her sleep, especially since we had to share a bed.

This is another media-perpetuated parenting myth: that co-sleeping with your young child is enjoyable. Sleeping in the same bed is not cute, nor is it sweet. Yet I still fall for it every time! There's nothing adorable about getting haymakered in the face at 2:00 a.m. or kicked in the throat because your kid somehow rotates their entire body upside down through the course of one night and insists on putting their dirty little kid feet as close to your mouth as possible. But I digress…

About 11:30 p.m., Em bolts upright and starts making the "I'm about to vomit" sound. Every kid's is slightly different, like a fingerprint. But every parent knows exactly what the cue is for their kid. I immediately calculated the distance to the bathroom—nope, not going to make it. I calculated the fallout of having to clean vomit off the hotel floor vs. in the bed itself. I tried to make out the features of her face in the dim room to see if I had enough time to grab a trash can. Nope, the only option was in the bed itself, so I tried to get her upright and aim it forward in between us so it missed Sean. My lovely husband, who, of course, was still mostly asleep and completely useless in the situation thus far.

For some reason, I thought it would be a good idea to grab a pillow. I can only blame that on the mysteries of being ripped from a blissfully unconscious state by the *horking* noise coming from my child's throat. I placed the pillow in front of her, somehow thinking if she only puked on the pillow, it would be easier to clean.

In what was a frighteningly close reenactment of the vomit scene from the movie *The Exorcist*, a stream of deep purple and red poured out of her mouth and hit the pillow square in the center of it. My moment of satisfaction at having provided an appropriate landing zone evaporated almost as instantaneously as I felt it when I realized the pillow was not so much a landing zone as a splash pad. At this point, Sean is finally fully awake and appropriately horrified. The stream of curse words coming from his mouth rivaled the vomit coming from Em's. For a few seconds, I sat there, frozen. My mind couldn't think fast enough about what to do, and she wasn't done anyway, so I had a moment or two to try and collect myself.

Eventually we got her cleaned up and removed the bedding. We realized it was a disaster of such epic proportions that we had to strip the bed all the way down to the mattress protector. I did the walk of shame to the hotel front desk and tried to explain the situation. The twenty-year-old behind the desk didn't even blink but wordlessly went and got a new set of bedding. I did have to request a few trash bags to put the linens in, and those were also provided without any sort of comment. It was at this moment I realized he thought I was utterly full of shit.

My brother lives in our hometown, which is a popular tourist destination for spring break, among other things. We were visiting during a peak season, and as the lobby doors opened behind me while I was waiting on my trash bags, two guys stumbled in. And I do mean actually stumbled. Weaving from side to side, one of them had his shirt mostly unbuttoned, and the other one seemed to have lost his shoes somewhere along the way. The second was mumbling something incoherent as the first one tried to aim his body in the general direction of the elevators. I am guessing the clerk thought I was bullshitting him with my story of "my kid puked in the bed" so I could cover for the fact that I had gone on a drunken vomiting spree of my own. I wish!

At this point, I didn't care and just wanted to be able to get everyone back to bed. Clean-up complete, we fell back asleep only to be awakened for round two approximately forty-five minutes later. In a total rookie move, I hadn't contemplated that she might possibly not have spewed out the entirety of the contents of her stomach. It sure as heck looked like she had! After that round was cleaned up, I abandoned my hopes of getting any rest for the remainder of the now-morning, put a bunch of towels on the bed, and tried to relax. Sure enough, round three followed closely thereafter, and at this point I was out of solutions as well as towels. Thankfully, three did seem to be the magic number, as that was the last round.

I cringed in the morning at the sight of the plastic bags and soiled linens outside the door. It's not that I was too concerned that most patrons of the hotel would attribute it to my inability to party without going overboard, although that's a highly likely assumption. I couldn't get it out of my head that some poor housekeeping team member somewhere had to deal with it.

On the off chance the events of the evening weren't exclusively blueberry-related, we decided to hit the road early to drive home. We packed up, checked out of the hotel, and headed for the highway. We were a few miles out of town when a small voice from the backseat piped up, "I'm hungry." Sean and I glanced at each other in terror, simultaneously calculating the hours until home. I started to reach for the cooler since fruit was always our go-to and quickly realized I wasn't willing to risk that.

"How about some crackers, honey?" I offered. "Sure, Mom," she agreed, distracted by the magical technologies of her tablet.

Good thing I'd packed eighty-seven other options besides blueberries.

Hijacked

———◆•◆———

5:32 a.m. I cracked my eyes open, took a luxurious stretch, then closed my eyes again to mentally envision my morning. After all, elite athletes use visualization to help them attain performance outcomes. I'm pretty sure I could use this to my advantage for this morning. I was getting up early to write! The house was quiet. Sean and Emersyn were both on spring break, so they could sleep in. I could get started, find my rhythm, and even enjoy a cup of coffee (yay previous-night-me for setting the coffee pot to auto-brew!) before the other members of Team Lance were even aware the sun had risen. Ahhh… I'd been waiting for this moment.

And then I heard it. The dreaded squeak of the door and turn of the handle coming out of Emersyn's room. She coughed her way over to my side of the bed. Allergy season is a bitch.

She flopped down next to me, coughed in my face three times for good measure, then proceeded to thrash around like an alligator being wrestled by Crocodile Dundee. This kid will not sleep with blankets on no matter what the temperature is, so I've learned to have an extra one on top of the covers that either she can get under so she doesn't wreck the sheets or so that I have a backup option for areas of my skin that are now mercilessly exposed to cold air. This morning it was option number two, so I reached for my emergency "Em is now in bed with me" blanket and started praying to the sleep gods this would be one of those times when she fell back asleep easily, and I could sneak out to get my writing in.

Of course, that wasn't in the cards.

She tossed. She turned. She coughed. She made snorting and throat-clearing noises that would make the crustiest of old men weep tears of pride. She finally settled down, and the tiny feathered thing of hope in my chest didn't quite sing but issued a single, hushed peep of possibility that perhaps my solo writing morning wouldn't be a total bust. And then I heard the dreaded words, "Mom, I have to pee."

Some nights I still wonder if someday Em will be sixteen years old and still asking me to come with her in the middle of the night. I realize this is the fuzzed-out, sleep-deprived early-morning thought of a mom who had other plans for how she wanted to spend her morning than being coughed on by a five-year-old who kicks off all the blankets, but it crossed my mind nonetheless. Moreover, the alarm bell in the back of my head starts ringing louder that I may not get to write at all. At this point, it was almost 6:00 a.m. It's now within a forty-five-minute window of Em's usual wake-up time, which means the likelihood of her going back to sleep is diminishing at a frightening speed.

We do the potty trip and get back into bed. I try to snug her closer to Sean to see if she'll gravitate towards him as her preferred parent of the morning (with no luck, of course), and I wait. And wait. And wait.

I mentally make one more hash mark on the wall, ticking off one more time that my expectation of dependable sleep and wake cycles was dashed against the rocks of the reality of parenting a small human. I surrender my desire for a solo writing session, kiss her forehead, and ask if she wants to keep snuggling or if she's ready to get up. Both her eyes fly open, wide with the hope of getting to watch TV since it's a no-school day. I smile and answer the question before she can ask it, trudging to stick my feet into my slippers while she shoots down the hallway like the little snot-rocket she is today.

I may not be penning any prose this morning, and while I'm grateful for the extra early-morning moments with my girl, I'm even more grateful to the overly optimistic previous-night me for the coffee.

Still a win.

I'm not sure why my brother felt the need to call me his "weird sister." This is probably also a good preview of about a million different times my older brother convinced me to do something in the name of play. I appreciate my mom's commitment to ensuring we were prepared for emergencies!

```
WHAT TO DO WHEN MOM PASSES OUT
(More conversations with Ian)

Ian: Mom, you're sitting on the barstool that Nickie took all the
little bolts out of. You're going to fall and hit your head.

Mom: And what would you do if I fell and passed out on the floor?

Ian: Get Daddy.

Mom: But what about times when Daddy's not here? Like now?

Nickie: I want another cookie.

Ian: I don't know.

Mom: Would you rush me off to the hospital?

Ian: No way.

Nickie: Another cookie? Please?

Mom: Well, you couldn't just leave me here. Do you remember how I
showed you how to call the operator?

Ian: Is that that funny voice that says "please hang up the phone"
when Nickie takes it off the hook?

Mom: Kind of. You pick up the phone and dial "0". A lady answers and
says "Operator. May I help you?"

Ian: Yeah-she sounds like she's talking in her nose.

Mom: Through her nose, not in it. Then what would you say?

Ian: My mom just fell off a barstool--

Mom: Just say my Mom is laying on the floor and won't talk to me.
Then she'll ask for your address. Do you remember it?

Ian: Ummmmmmm. Yeah! One, six,.....

Mom: No! Five, three...

Ian: Oh yeah! Three five oh...

Mom: No! Five, three...

Nickie: You always give Ian cookies and never me!

Ian: South Palo Birdie.

Mom: 530 South Palo VERDE not birdie.

Nickie: Mom where is my blue bird that squeaks?

Mom: Okay, Ian, then she'll ask who else is in the house with you.
What will you say?
```

Ian: Just me and my weird sister Nickie who's two.

Nickie: That's not very nice Ian. Mom, Ian called me weird.

Mom: Then the operator will say "We'll send out an ambulance right away" and you hang up the phone.

Ian: Okay. I say "Please send an ambliance for my mom who's on the floor" and they'll send one?

Mom: Yes. But this is only for an emergency, when no one is around.

Ian: Is that the same place the pizzas come from?

Mom: No! That's a restaurant that delivers pizza.

Ian: Would they pick up Nickie if she was on the floor and couldn't talk also?

Mom: Yes....if it was an emergency.

Ian: Come on, Nick. Let's go play in my room. You lay down on the floor....don't talk, now....

Kindergarten Field Trips

When it comes to school support, I'm highly proficient at purchasing snacks and donating supplies. Volunteering with a bunch of five and six-year-olds eager to touch, sneeze, breathe, and possibly fart on me? Not so much.

For most of Em's kindergarten year, I gave myself a pass on volunteering in the classroom. I told the teacher from the beginning I would be an excellent supporter when it came to classroom donations and needed purchases, and I came through on that commitment. I don't know if it was because it was getting down to the last few weeks of school or because my daughter wore me down by asking when I was going to come volunteer in her classroom "like Daddy did" or what, but I caved and signed up for two time slots of in-room volunteering along with chaperoning her field trip to the zoo.

Before I go further, to be fair, I'd like to clarify that my wonderful husband did, indeed, volunteer in her classroom. He's a high school teacher, so it's tough for him to get time off to do things like that. One time, back in the fall, he came in with multiple other parents and helped out with the class Halloween party. Before I go even further, to be fair to myself, I also basically shamed and bullied him into it in a moment of my own anxiety.

He hadn't been able to make her Student of the Month award ceremony, and since he coached girls' wrestling, he was going to be gone most nights and pretty much every weekend for almost four months. I freaked out about him being gone and the long-term psychological effects of that on her development and, essentially, made him feel terrible if he didn't volunteer for the Halloween party. (Yes, looking back now, I'm probably thinking the same thing you are, but that's for my therapist to help me sort out.) Anyway, despite my best efforts at being present, taking her to evening and even weekend school events, "Daddy volunteered in my classroom, and you didn't" had become an increasingly frequent refrain.

I run my own business and travel fairly frequently, and due to the nature of my work, my schedule is consistently unpredictable. I found myself looking at a few weeks in a row where I was going to have availability, so I emailed her teacher and asked to sign up.

Full disclosure: I canceled the first slot.

The week came around, and I realized I'd be in her room two weeks in a row and then chaperoning an all-day field trip that third week. Emails were piling up, and I was starting to get a bit stressed, so I bailed.

And, no, I don't feel bad about it. It was an excellent decision and a highly productive afternoon.

The time came around for the first volunteering slot (the one I was actually going to show up for), which was only two hours in the afternoon before school was dismissed. "I can do two hours!" I thought to myself. I showed up, had my "time to have fun with a class full of kindergarteners" mindset ready to go, and headed to the classroom. We adored her teacher, and she was all smiles as she greeted me. She then informed me the kids were in "P.E." for another forty minutes and asked if I'd help her with some preparatory work for their notebooks. That took me about ten minutes, and we ended up kind of chit-chatting for the other thirty.

I felt like an asshole for not even knowing the schedule so I could have come at a different time! She assured me it was a testing day, so it was a little more off than usual. The time finally rolled around for the kids to come back to the classroom, and I walked with her to get them. I was prepared for my child to be excited and for there to be lots of attention and excitement.

I was not prepared for the amount of tiny, grubby kindergarten hands that would touch me or how close they would be to my face when they talked to me. I'm pretty sure 90% of the class breathed directly into my mouth.

Volunteer time turned out to be more fun than I was fearing. I got to read with a smaller group of the kids and play a word bingo game. The best part was the huge smile on Em's face the whole time. It was definitely time well-invested. At the same an afternoon, if I'm being brutally honest, it also affirmed my decision through most of the year to not spend my time this way. I love my kid, hell, I even love the other kids in her class, and I also know that I'm not exactly wired for those interactions.

This, of course, amped my anxiety about the impending zoo trip.

There was no way I was backing out of that one, so I steeled myself and mustered up as much excitement as I could. I focused on the memories I was making with my kid and the fact I could make life a little easier for her teacher. I walked into school feeling pretty good about it. We had our group assignments, and I'd only be responsible for four of the kids. I'd already met two of the three children besides my own who'd be joining our small group, and THANK GOD, another parent was meeting us there to help out as well.

One of my greatest fears is wrangling kids, especially those who aren't my own. I can speak in front of groups of thousands of adults and not miss a beat, but put me in with tiny little opinionated humans who don't listen to directions, need steady supplies of snacks and bathroom breaks with little to no warning? Abject terror.

I plastered my chaperone badge onto my t-shirt, and walked to the kindergarten room. Every ounce of my fear and concern melted away the second Em yelled, "Mommy!" and came bouncing over.

My anxiety promptly returned as we began to get the directions for the day. For some reason, I thought the whole class would stay together as we navigated the zoo, and there would be a plan for what we were going to see and do. Nope! Each group of four kids plus their chaperone were on their own with vague directions like "meet near the entrance for lunch around 11:30 a.m." and "be back by where the buses dropped us off by 1:00 p.m." As someone who is directionally challenged and has a hard time finding her way back to any sort of starting point, this furthered my fears, but I figured I could maybe just tag along with another group and ride it out that way.

Of course this was nothing like what actually happened. I'd underestimated the pace at which a small group of kindergarteners could move. We were definitely on our own, and again, I whispered prayers of gratitude for the other parent who joined our little group. He had experience doing this with his older kids, so I had a reasonable amount of assurance that we'd all survive the trip intact.

Things went smoothly for the first few hours. Well, smoothly in terms of nobody falling into the alligator pond, only two scraped knees, four or five minor tussles over who got to go first, and about ninety-seven complaints about being hot and thirsty. I was counting it all as a win until things started to unravel when we still had about an hour and fifteen minutes before the trip was over.

"Miss Lance, I want to go home. When can I go home? I don't want to be here anymore." One of the little boys in the group was toast. He was tired, hot, and completely uninterested in the zoo any longer. We were about a million miles from the meet-up point with the buses, so even if I wanted to just plop down and take a break for a while, the fact of the matter was that we needed to make up some mileage to get us back to where we needed to be. "Pretty soon, man!" I chirped. "Ooh, look, we're right by the orangutans!"

I may not know much about kids, but I do know whining is contagious, and I was trying to prevent this plague from spreading. This little boy also happened to be my daughter's best friend (she would have referred to him as her future husband, but I told her she had to wait a few decades for that), so I was especially worried Em would pick up this thread. And when Em starts whining, it all falls apart. The orangutan was a successful distraction for a few minutes, but the second we were back on the trail, I felt a pull on my hand, "Miss Lance. NOW can we go home? I don't want to be here anymore."

At this point, I desperately wanted to be empathetic. I felt for the kid, truly. I offered some words of encouragement, showed him the time on my phone, and provided an updated countdown, "Only sixty-seven minutes left! It's going to go fast!" Next up was the tiger enclosure, and I prayed to the gods of massive cats that this would give me the pivot point we needed.

I'm pretty sure the tiger gods each held up one giant furry paw with their middle claws fully extended, because it was at that moment that the kids spotted the tiger statue and decided they all wanted to climb on it. The problem was that my daughter, who had truly been pretty much a trooper the whole trip, decided she was done and activated her "only child" setting to the nth degree. I heard her little voice raise in pitch, "I want to go first!" She was not interested in taking turns. She did not want to wait. She did not want to share. She did not want to go after her friends. She did not want to be part of the team.

I tried to get a group picture of everyone since they were all bunched up on it anyway in hopes we could do that and then nicely take turns so each kid (mostly aimed at avoiding my own child's impending emotional implosion) could get their own solo picture. Nope. Em was having none of that nonsense. The best picture I have shows three smiling kindergarteners hanging off the tiger statue and my kiddo in the back with arms angrily crossed and a deep scowl on her face. Her displeasure was clear.

At this point, we still had about half a million miles to walk back to the meeting place, so I was trying to rally my little troops while navigating my daughter's emotional distress. We walked along, and the best way she could express it was, "I don't want to have any friends here anymore! I want to be alone so I can be first!"

Same, baby girl, same.

With my daughter angry and scowling, one kid near tears because of the unfairness of having to stay at the zoo when he just wanted to go home, one girl repeatedly losing her hair bows because she kept taking them out after I put them back in but refusing to let me hold them so she wouldn't keep losing them, and one kid blessedly being taken care of by his dad, we finally made it back to the meeting spot.

A few hours later, ensconced on the couch with an ice cream treat, I kissed my daughter on the forehead, and she beamed up at me, "That was the best day ever, Mom. When can we do it again?"

I chose not to tell her that Mommy was planning on taking a break from chaperoning field trips for a few more years. Like maybe thirteen of them.

Chaos and Cleo

Remember back in the "Oreo 2.0" chapter when I so assuredly stated I did not have time or capacity to take care of a four-legged family member which required time, attention, and exercise?

So much for that idea.

I'd never completely given up on my idea of getting another dog. We had to put my Nala down in October of 2020. Between a miscarriage in January 2020, the COVID-19 pandemic, and saying goodbye to my four-legged best friend, it was a hell of a year. It took me a long time to grieve, and of course, in the midst of it all, I was navigating early childhood years with Em and all the other aspects of life. Healing was slow, but this past year as the holidays rolled around, I started contemplating the idea of finding a dog who would fit our family again. The prior Christmas, we had tried to adopt a sweet little two-year-old rescue pup that some friends of mine had saved. Unfortunately, she wasn't a good fit with Emersyn, so we helped the young dog get to an amazing home where she fit perfectly.

This year, however, I found myself looking at photos of corgi puppies. I've wanted a corgi since I was a little kid, but of course, it never "made sense." They're expensive, we're supposed to adopt from shelters, etc. The reality in our house was that if we were going to get a dog, we would need to get a puppy so it could bond with Em. Getting a puppy is another thing I swore wholeheartedly I would never do, yet again, there I was, gearing up for exactly that adventure. I was mindlessly scrolling corgi puppy pictures, considering whether or not we could possibly add this to the mix, when Em plopped down beside me before I could put my phone away. "I WANT TO SEE PUPPY PICTURES!" she shrieked in delight.

For the next five minutes, we not only looked at corgi pictures, but I decided to "just do a little research" and looked up breeders in our area so I could see when they might have litters available. Of course, these breeders know what they're doing, so there were quite a few options for litters that would oh-so-conveniently be available just before the winter holidays. I was looking at one set of puppies in particular and wasn't paying too much attention to Emersyn when all of a sudden she burst into tears. Not little tears, either, but a giant sob and full-on tears rolling down her face. "Baby, what's the matter?" I asked with some measure of alarm as I turned towards her.

"They're…just…sooo…CUTE," she wailed as she threw herself into my arms. The poor little thing was totally overcome, and of course, I felt the same way, but about her. (Ok, and about the puppies, too.) I didn't know it was possible for my heart to sink and soar at the same time, but it was clear that we were about to embark on the adventure of getting a puppy.

I'd never had a puppy before. My dog was already six years old when I adopted her, so I wasn't quite sure what to expect. I mean, I'd given birth to and managed to keep a tiny human alive for five years at this point, so I was pretty sure I could manage it, but there were also so many things I didn't know. Per my usual approach, I turned to the internet. That lasted about five minutes before I shut it all down, realizing there was no amount of research that would help me feel totally great about this decision. We were going to need to commit and figure it out as we went. It was time for Em to start getting ready for school, and Sean emerged just as I was sending her off to get dressed. "Daddy, we're getting a puppy! A CORGI PUPPY!" she announced elatedly. Sean flicked his eyes to me as if to communicate, "Do you want to disappoint her, or should I do it?"

I took a breath and tried to keep my gaze steady, "Yep, it's time. We can get this one before Christmas," I said as I turned my phone towards him. I credit my husband's steady, unflappable nature for retaining his hold on his coffee cup. I'd been laying the groundwork for this conversation, and of course, we had the failed adoption attempt of the prior holiday season in our back pockets, so it wasn't a total and complete shock. That being said, I'm pretty sure he thought I would kick the can down the road at least until summer vacation. But nope! Now I'd committed, and Em was excited. We weren't just on the road to adopting a puppy; we were racing down it full throttle.

Fast forward six weeks, and we were driving to Chino Valley (Cheeto Valley, according to Em) to pick up our pup. We'd decided to name her Cleo, and Em couldn't wait to meet her. By this point, my more rational, practical side had kicked in and I wasn't exactly regretting the decision but was certainly having second, third, and fourth thoughts about the situation. Despite all that, we arrived at the pick-up location and went in to meet our girl. The family brought her out, and Emersyn sank to her knees as they put the puppy in front of her. Cleo immediately licked her face, and Em got teary again. I teared up a bit, too, if I'm being honest. We got in the car, and although I'd spent a ridiculous amount of money on a little puppy container for Cleo to ride in safely, she, of course, immediately wormed her way right out of it and sat on Emersyn's lap instead.

The hour-and-a-half-long drive passed in a blink, and before I knew it, we were home. Not dissimilar to having a baby, it was at this point I realized, "I really have no fucking idea what we're doing." It's kind of that thing that you know is true, but you don't realize how true it is until you are in your own living room, thinking of all the things you never knew you needed to consider about what needs to be done to take care of this tiny thing. A million paper towels, two bottles of cleaning spray, and approximately 175 puppy pee pads later, we'd survived the first few months. We'd figured out crate training, first veterinarian appointments, and which food gave her runny diarrhea that required outside potty trips every 90 minutes all night.

Early on in this adventure I coined the phrase, "Chaos and Cleo." Chaos didn't necessarily refer to Emersyn, although there are times that is most certainly true. It's more about the amount of chaos this tiny little puppy created, not just in our house but in our schedule. The chaos of me trying to work from home and keep an eye on her, but realizing that if I leave her in the crate or pen in the living room she would cry and bark, and if I put the pen in my office, she'd pee and try to chew the carpet while I was in the middle of a coaching call. It was realizing we needed to figure out how to travel with her and keep her from trying to jump into the front seat as I was driving. It was all the amazing, wonderful, beautiful, loud laughter coming from my daughter as she raced around with Cleo.

There are messes. There is dog hair. LOTS of dog hair. There have been stolen headbands from Emersyn's stash, and toys pilfered from the playroom. More than one doll has lost a hand or been on the receiving end of puppy teeth chew marks. Cleo will dig through a basket of laundry until she finds the exact sock she'd prefer to steal. There have been spills and carpet poops and midnight trips outside to potty. There was also one epic event of stolen pizza from the top of the hot tub when we realized Cleo's parkour skills far exceeded the proportions of her stubby legs.

Literally as I'm writing this, Cleo has managed to jump up to the top of the couch and is walking around it, trying to chew the cords on the window and peek inside the stand-up lamp to see if there are any moths she can eat. My dear husband, who decidedly did not want the puppy but was begrudgingly willing to go along with it, has spent more time laying on the floor playing with her, shuffling his feet around corners to play chase with her, and gives me the most self-satisfied, smug look every time Cleo hops up to sit with him on his chair. This would be the same husband who insisted the dog was not, I repeat NOT, allowed on the couch. This is the same husband who was also the first one to break that rule.

I'm not sure how we did it, but somehow, we managed to adopt a pup that has the same personality as our daughter. It's almost comical, from the infamous corgi side-eye to her dramatics, the similarities are striking. It's undeniable that she and Em share that special bond that some puppies and kids form. It's also indisputable that bringing this four-legged furry friend into the family has created a whole new level of chaos for Team Lance.

We're here for it.

I can only imagine what was going through my mom's head during THIS conversation…

```
CONVERSATIONS WITH IAN AND NICK

ON PROFANITY

IAN: Uh-oh, Nickie, don't let Mom hear you say that!
MOM: Say what??
NICKIE: NOTHING!
MOM: Ian, tell me what she said.
NICKIE: I didn't say it! Ian said it! Ian said it!!
IAN: I said it, but Nickie said it, too!!
NICKIE: I didn't really say it! Not as loud as Ian!!
IAN: You did, too!
MOM: Stop it! Someone tell me what you said!
NICKIE: Uh-oh, Ian. I think we're in deeeeeep trouble!
IAN: I can't say it, Mom. It's too bad. You'll KILL me.
MOM: I won't kill you. Tell me what you said. NOW!
IAN: Oh, Mom, I can't. I can't say it. Please don't make me.
NICKIE: That's right, Mom, he can't say it. It's TERRIBLE!
MOM: Is it something you heard at school?
IAN: I can't tell you! I can't say it!
MOM: Ian, this is ridiculous. I'm giving you permission to tell
me the word so that I can explain it to you and tell you why
it's bad. It's probably something silly that someone said and you
just don't realize it. NOW TELL ME!
IAN: Do you promise you won't beat me???
MOM: Yes, I promise I won't beat you like I do all the time.
IAN: Oooohh, you're gonna be mad. I don't think I can say it.
NICKIE: Go ahead, Ian! Say it! She'll just yell a little bit!
MOM: Okay, Ian, SPELL it then.
IAN: Okay, here goes. You promised you won't get mad, now....
The first letter is C.
MOM: And the next? (frantic thoughts of filthy "C" words)
Ian: U.
MOM: (Dear Lord, why is John NEVER home at times like these?)
Go ahead, Ian. (I'll be calm. I won't throw a fit.)
IAN: You promised, Mom, remember! The next letter is S!
```

MOM: S?

IAN: Are you mad? I know you're mad! You're going to kill me!!!

MOM: Ian, I don't even know the stupid word yet! WHAT IS IT?

IAN: Okay, I'll say it! It's CUSS!

MOM: (Cuss--spelled r-e-l-i-e-f) That's not a bad word! That means to swear, to say a bad word! It's not a bad word by itself. That's why I wanted you to tell me what it was. Now you know what it means.

IAN: Wow, am I glad. I thought I was in big trouble.

NICKIE: Mom, I know!! I'll tell you ALL the bad words I know and you can tell me what they mean, okay?

MOM: Not a chance, Nick.

Kindergarten Promotion

My daughter has spent the majority of her now-six years on this planet firmly convinced of two things: pink is the best color, and dresses or skirts are the best outfit choices. Until this morning.

Today is kindergarten promotion day. We've been looking forward to this for weeks. Counting down the days while trying to manage the myriad year-end activities, dress-up days, and end-of-year school activities, along with her birthday. It's been a lot, but we finally made it. Sunday night was spent picking out the perfect dress so Monday morning could be smooth.

So much for that idea.

She slept in quite a bit later than usual, which isn't a bad thing. I used the extra time to get a few things done and prepare for my own day. I felt good about the time because we'd already gotten the outfit ready and had a plan for lunch. I heard her little feet shuffling down the hall and chuckled as Cleo shot herself off the blanket where she was lounging and barreled down the hall to greet Em like she does every morning. Emersyn gave Cleo some love and what looked a bit like a wobbly smile, then promptly burst into tears.

With no context and also my own experiences that sometimes the day just starts out this way, I wrapped her up in a big, long hug and made the huge mistake of suggesting we get dressed. You'd think after six years I could read the signs a bit better, but oh no. That sent her into a tailspin, complete with a face plant onto the couch and a fresh wave of tears.

"I don't want to wear the sunflower dress!" she wailed. (I'm pretty sure there was also gnashing of teeth, but I wasn't going close enough to that trainwreck of kindergarten emotion to check.) "Ok, you don't have to wear the dress. You can pick something else, no problem!" I replied, trying to set my cheer factor at the appropriate level to be encouraging but not overwhelmingly so. Her little brow furrowed and arms crossed, "I'm wearing this," she declared.

I'm pretty lax about pajama rules—we have a few sets, but when it comes to what she wears to bed, as long as she goes to sleep, I could give two shits about what she wears. Last night, however, her ensemble was an old pair of black shorts that she'd pretty much already outgrown and that were practically see-through because they'd been worn and washed so many times. She's currently in a phase where she's refusing to wear underwear except for when we force her to wear them if we're leaving the house, so those weren't included. The shirt was a pink tank top that had a cartoon drawing of a red panda on it that she'd had for about a year and a half. Since she got it, she referred to it as her "corgi tank top," and no one has ever been able to convince her it's a red panda and not a corgi, so we just refer to it as that.

The corgi tank top was once bright pink but has faded with washings as well. At some point she also managed to stick a fabric label on the front of it, just over the poor panda/corgi's ear, and while the label itself is no longer there, the residue has remained and has collected enough black and gray fuzz that it just looks like this odd rectangle of old sticky stuff. Hence why I don't mind it for bed, but it usually doesn't make an appearance if we're going to school.

I drew my usual line at underwear and also reminded her that the students were asked to "dress to impress" (the teacher's words, not mine) for promotion day, so could we please find some decent pants or a nice skirt or a dress and we could put the tank top over the top of it? She asked for her gold sequin skirt, and I immediately agreed and said I thought it was an excellent fancy choice and that I would go get it from the living room. Before I could even go get it, she saw her other sequin skirt lying in the heap of stuffed animals at the end of her bed. This is the same exact skirt, but it's covered in hot pink sequins. At this point, I heard the pitch of her little voice rise an octave higher, and she grabbed the skirt, forcefully exclaiming, "I'm not wearing this skirt! I don't like pink! Pink is an awful color!"

I teach communication for a living, so my de-escalation training kicked in. I lowered the pitch of my own voice, keeping a calm tone and being sure to end on a down note, "I agree. I like the gold one. I'll go get it for you." Meanwhile, I prayed to the parenting gods to shower me with mercy and was utterly and immediately denied said mercy. Em teared up again and flung herself onto the rocking chair in her room, vehemently affirming she was NOT wearing a skirt. I offered a pair of flowy pink and orange pants as pretty much our only acceptable alternative if we wanted anything that looked remotely "nice," and she immediately sat up and said, "Ooh, yeah. I love those pink stripes, and there's orange, too!"

No, I did not point out the color conflict from her previous statement.

We got into the bathroom to do her hair, and I realized the tank top was so stretched out it's not going to be appropriate for school. Luckily for me, Em agreed and even laughed about it. I will take a pause here to also state that in the middle of the melee, it occurred to me she could possibly be hungry, so I had been shoving in bites of strawberries and blueberries between tantrums. I am convinced that's the only thing that kept us sort of on track. We headed back to her room to face the dreaded closet once again.

Even the fruit wasn't enough for this point. She pitched herself onto the bed and threw her arms out wide, aiming a glare directly at me. "You know, Mom. At the spring concert, all of my other friends—well, maybe not all ALL of them, but most of them, or at least a lot of them—they all had long dresses. And you don't ever ever ever ever ever ever ever ever ever EVER get me long dresses."

At this point, I was watching the minutes drain off the clock and out of my life forever. Cleo was intermittently chewing on Emersyn's shoes that were scattered about the floor and impossibly tiny pieces of Barbie doll-related debris as I again attempted de-escalation. "I know; I was surprised by that, too. They were very pretty. You have two long dresses and also a long skirt—would you like to wear one of those?"

I mean, has there been a worse suggestion in the entire history of the known universe? Not according to my kid, there hasn't. I started flipping through options, avoiding eye contact and the "melt your soul death stare" that was boring into my back. I figured we could find a different shirt to wear with the pants, or maybe something else would catch her eye. And, of course, I was right! A few hanger flips in, Em bursts out, "Oh, I love that one! Can I wear that one, Mama?" in a sugar-sweet voice.

Lo and behold, it's one of the long dresses to which I had just referred and which had just been vehemently shot down by the fashionista herself. I abandoned any desire to be right a long time ago, so I immediately affirmed the choice, ripped her tank top off and yanked her pants down, tossed the dress over her head, added a quick pair of shorts underneath it, and held up a pair of shoes. By some small miracle, I nailed the shoe choice on the first go. A very cute pair of yellow (pink is soooo last year) sandals with a cut-out flower design. It took a minute to find the right pair of socks, but luckily, the purple and white unicorn pair came to the rescue.

Then we traipsed into the bathroom for hair. Or at least I tried to get us to traipse into the bathroom for hair.

In the midst of mornings like these, I sometimes forget that my child gets overwhelmed when faced with a lot of options. If I'm being completely truthful, when I get rattled, I have a tendency to fire things off like a drill sergeant giving orders to new recruits. We were headed out of her room when I blasted her with hair options. "You want two braids today? A full braid? A half bun with half down? Bubble braid?" Much to my dismay, she veered away from the bathroom and stomped into the living room, now flinging herself on our much-abused couch. There really was an excessive amount of bodily flinging happening this morning.

She covered her face with her hands as even more tears made an encore appearance. Still trying to be kind as she was obviously having a tough morning, and I may not have helped it by offering so many options all at once, I simply clasped my hands together and said, "Oh baby, what can I do to help you feel better?" Now, this is where a lot of the parenting tactics will tell you the child will respond to empathy, productive dialogue will occur, and you'll repair and reset and move on with your lives.

Not with my kid. At least not this morning.

At this point, Emersyn removed her hands from her face slowly. She took a deep breath, obviously trying to gain composure. And then she looked at me like I was the world's most giant dumbass, and in the single most condescending tone I've ever been on the receiving end of, she began to explain it in words that it seemed she could only hope a simpleton like me could understand.

"Mom. All of my other friends get really cool hairstyles. I only ever wear my hair down. Especially on days when something is important. I don't ever ever ever ever ever ever wear it any other way."

Now, at this point, I was lulled into a very brief but very blissful false sense of security. "Ah!" I thought to myself. "This will be easy. I'm just an idiot for not remembering that she likes to wear it down for big event days. I got this!"

She continued, "I always want my hair to look cool like my friends. But you never ever ever ever ever ever EVER give me a cool hairstyle." More tears erupted. At this point, I was about out of patience, I snapped into my mom voice and said, "That's what I'm literally standing here trying to offer you. How about a bubble braid?"

We settled on a fucking bubble braid and made it out the door two minutes later, Emersyn happily chattering about how much she was looking forward to the day.

At that point I texted my husband two things that were equally true: that bubble braid wasn't going to last past the second period of the day, and even though it was Monday morning, I was ready for an adult beverage.

Croc Tops, Coffee, and Conclusions

It's 5:28 a.m. Coffee is almost done brewing. The puppy is—at least for now—not chewing on anything she's not supposed to. I've got my manuscript notes ready to go, and I'm going to finish this book. I stepped outside for a few minutes of silence and gratitude after I got out of bed. I thought of my mom and how excited she would be for me. I did a quick reflection on the journey of writing this book and shook my head at the miracle of actually finishing it. I'm so excited to complete this part of the adventure.

Settled in on the couch, I arranged my blanket just so and was just about to open my computer when I heard the heart-wrenching creak of the bedroom door.

"You've got to be freaking kidding me," I thought in desperation as Cleo tore down the hallway to see if her favorite little human was finally awake. Of course this is what would happen this morning.

Em joined me in bed last night at about 3:00 a.m. after another alleged nightmare. I say alleged because I'm pretty sure she only woke up to go to the bathroom, but she's figured out how to game the system and knows that if she tells me she had a nightmare, I'll usually either come lay down with her or, on occasions when I'm too exhausted to adhere to better parenting practices that will encourage my child to sleep in her own space, I let her come sleep with me. Last night was definitely the latter, mostly because I was anticipating an early morning writing session and didn't want to lose too much time trying to coax her into sleeping in her own bed.

She shuffles down the hallway and emerges into the living room, tummy on full display and rubbing at her eyes in the early morning light. About two weeks ago, she started in on me about wanting a "croc top" shirt. Despite my efforts to educate her that the term is, in fact, crop top, Em vehemently denies any accuracy of my knowledge and continues to refer to them as croc tops. To my dismay, crop tops have made a comeback and are everywhere, including in small sizes for girls her age. While I am a proponent of her making her own fashion choices, midriffs at six years old is a trend I'm not ready to support for my own kid. This might be a continual battle for the next twelve years, but it's a position I'm willing to staunchly defend at this point.

And by staunchly I mean I 100% caved and made her a deal.

I was not willing to spend money on a crop top, and she wouldn't be allowed to wear it out of the house or in front of anybody else besides me and her dad, but I would make her one from a shirt she already owned. She selected a shirt from her wardrobe, and I cut off the bottom half. I figured she'd get tired of wearing it after a few days, but I seriously underestimated my daughter's enjoyment of having her belly button on full display. In the sixteen days since I made her the damn croc top, she's worn it about twelve of those days for approximately twenty of the twenty-four hours of each day. The exceptions have been when we went out of town and I happened to "forget" to pack it, and when we forced her to put on other clothing to leave the house. I think I've only washed it twice.

At this point, the coffee is done and my mug is loaded. I've got Emersyn snuggled on the couch next to me, futilely hoping she would magically drift back off to sleep. "Aha!" I think. This is perfect. I've been wanting to read my book to Em to get her reaction. I mean, I've spent the better part of a year working on this project, laughing and crying over stories of her. It wouldn't exist without her, and I'm excited to see what she thinks.

I've tried this two other times since I completed the majority of the first draft, thinking it might be fun to share some of the book with her before it gets published. I wanted to let her in on the process of what I'd been creating and how much she inspired it. I wanted to make sure she knew that even though she never got to meet Grandma Sherry, she was still part of our lives and certainly part of this adventure. Maybe Emersyn would like to hear some other things my Mom wrote about me or some of the funny stories I'd captured about Emersyn herself. Knowing my child, the self-interest aspects would probably be the more likely option.

For my first attempt, I was sitting on the couch with my manuscript at the ready. The first full printed copy of the rough draft. I caught Emmy's eye while she was in the middle of playing and asked if she might want to hear some of what I'd written. "It's a book about you, Em!" I exclaimed. "I've written down a bunch of stories of all the cool things you've done or funny things you've said. Would you like to hear some of them?"

Ever opportunistic and seeing an opening to once again badger me for more TV time, my nearly impossible-to-impress child didn't miss a beat, nor did she even make full eye contact. She simply responded, "No thanks. Can I watch *Bluey*?"

My second attempt came when we were out at dinner as a family. I figured I would have a captive audience, and she'd be willing to at least commit to listening to it at some point since we didn't have much else going on. I asked if she'd like to hear some of the book I'd written about her when we got home later. She met my eyes for a millisecond, muttered a noncommittal and wholly unexcited "Sure," and immediately went back to playing with her sticker book.

A few hours later that night, we were getting ready to start the bedtime routine. I was working on some edits to the book, so I thought maybe this would finally be the right time for my desired mother/daughter bonding over my writing project. My husband was sitting in the chair across the room from us, and he'd been expressing excitement and anticipation of hearing some of what I'd written. My magical family moment had arrived.

"You guys want to hear some of the book now?" I asked. "Sure, Mom!" Emmy replied, my zeal for sharing waning rapidly as she immediately rushed off down the hall after Cleo. I figured I'd start reading and would capture their attention that way. About two sentences in, I glanced up and noticed my husband's eyes firmly glued to the TV screen. Em was running laps down the hallway, through the kitchen, around the dining table, and zooming back through the living room with Cleo barking at her and nipping at her heels the whole time. I decided to keep going and read the rest of the page. I'm pretty sure Em gave me her full attention for a grand total of two seconds. I did get at least half of Sean's attention.

I'm hoping Cleo was impressed.

But with today's early wake-up and a quiet house, I finally had my captive audience. "Em, how about I read you some of the book I've been writing about you, and you can snuggle in and maybe go back to sleep?" I asked softly, tucking in the fuzzy blanket around her as she wormed her way next to me on the couch. "Ok, Mommy," she said with a yawn.

I did an internal fist pump and quick shimmy of delight that I'd finally get my chance to share this special moment with her and cracked open my computer. I started with some parts of the letter I wrote to her at the beginning of the book, but she seemed more interested in the fringe on the blanket than what I was reading. I switched to the story about her starting kindergarten, which got a similar lack of reaction. My hope drying up as fast as my dreams of a quiet house had, I opted for Fingus/Felix and Pickle Cheese, thinking I could engage her by talking about her friends more directly. It could be that I finally had her attention, or she was still not awake enough to realize she had other options besides listening to me, but she was still and attentive while I finished. "So, what did you think, baby?"

"I like it, but I don't really like it."

Hear that "eeeeee" noise? That's the sound of my proverbial balloon being popped and the air leaking out of it slowly.

"Huh," I said. "Well, what would make you like it more?" I inquired, a bit fearful of what her answer would be.

"A puppy video, Mommy. Watching puppy videos makes me feel happy with books."

"Em, how can you watch a video if you're supposed to be reading the book? That's not the point," I countered.

"You watch the video, and whenever it's over, you can read the book," she replied with a hefty dose of incredulity at my idiocy. Uncharacteristically, I couldn't come up with a new way to try and redirect the conversation that had gone off the rails, so I looked at her silently. She blinked a few times and finally uttered, "Please just listen to me."

Her tone of voice made it crystal clear that what she truly meant was, "Please just listen to me…you dumb fuck."

In one last-ditch attempt to resurrect my hoped-for moment of bonding, I stated, "You seem to be wanting to watch puppy videos instead of reading my book I wrote about you." I didn't even get to my next sentence before Em, fully exasperated with me now, burst out, "Yes. And you're being rude. Can you please go get your phone now?"

At least she said please.

Having a kid is a trip. It is the wildest of wild rides and the most adventurous adventure I could imagine. The daily emotional rollercoaster shoots me from smiling and laughing to wanting to vomit at a neck-breaking pace. Em makes me laugh and brings me more joy and more peace than anything I've ever experienced. She also jacks up my blood pressure faster than anything I've ever experienced.

Motherhood as a biological mom wasn't something I ever expected for myself. I sure as hell wasn't anticipating it in my later thirties. Now, as an early elementary parent in my forties, I know enough to know I have zero clue of what the coming years will hold. I do know that I will continue to love my little one fiercely, and I will do what it takes to be the best mom for Emersyn that I possibly can.

If I reflect back to the version of me who was bawling about being pregnant and missing wine and then forecast forward to who I might be a few more years from now, it's an incredible journey.

Reflecting on all the adventures and challenges since then, I'm amazed at my own growth.

There may not be many nights in the hot tub with martinis after she's gone to bed like I thought there might be, but I wouldn't trade it for the world.

Dear Mom

Dear Mom,

You played a critical role in this book. Discovering your typed words and stories from my childhood certainly brought in a missing element that I was able to incorporate, but it was much more than that.

I distinctly remember conversations with you as you talked about writing a book someday. I have vivid memories of these discussions, thinking that if anyone could write an amazing book, it would have been you. I also remember being somewhat shocked by and eventually hugely interested in the idea that writing a book was an adventure I could possibly have as well. You never got to accomplish your dream, but this is now my second book, and I feel you with me each step of the way.

Don't get me wrong, I'm still pissed you're not here to help with things like school drop-off or birthday party planning. You can't meet me for happy hour so I can bemoan the latest tantrum Emersyn threw or whining fit we had to endure. I can't text you for support or ask your advice to find out what worked with me when I was growing up.

I'm sure you'd be laughing—and probably shaking your head, too—at Em's antics. You'd affirm our similarities and shake your head knowingly as I shared my latest frustrations and favorite stories. I have to think that if you and I could survive my childhood, Em and I stand a pretty good chance of making it, too. Can you even imagine what the next six years will hold? I know I can't.

Thanks for giving me the foundation I needed to start this journey. I love you.

-Niki

Dear Emersyn

Dear Emersyn,

Ok, you little supernova of a human being. We made it. More or less intact, too! Whew!

Thank you for being you. Despite our occasional clash of the titans when your giant personality goes up against mine and the frequent "angry eyes" stare you level at me, we make a good team. I couldn't ask for a better partner. You encourage and challenge me on the regular. You test my patience and inspire me. You make me laugh, shake my head, and want to scream, often all in the same interaction. You're a mirror for me, and nothing I've ever experienced has prompted me to grow as much as you do.

It's tempting to write, "I hope you never change!" But that wouldn't be true. I hope we help you learn to sleep deeply and regularly. I hope we move out of the whining phase because it's oh-so-annoying. I hope you cultivate a practice of picking up the damn playroom. I hope you continue to develop your own interests and talents. I hope you come to love bedtime someday so I can enjoy the hot tub again.

I also hope you don't change at all because you're YOU. I hope you keep this same stubbornly fierce commitment to your independence. You don't care what other people think. Hell, you barely care what I think! And as frustrating as that can be for us sometimes, it's so utterly perfect. Your dad and I have thrown out the phrase "Strong, independent woman" about you since we first brought you home from the hospital, and you fought to hold your own bottle in just those first few weeks. I hope this is always true for you.

Thanks for the journey so far. I have a feeling there are many more chapters to be written!

I love you.
Mom

Appreciations

Sean - we did it! Thank you for your endless support, coffee refills, encouragement, and adult beverage delivery when required. Your belief in me never wavers, and I am beyond grateful for you. Thanks for being such an important part of this whole adventure with me!

Emersyn, Em, Emmy, Em the Gem, Emmybear - thank you for being you and for reminding me to stop and play along the way! (Or at least forcing me to because you wouldn't leave me alone when I was trying to write)

Dad - thank you for always being one of my biggest fans. I loved watching you read an early rough draft. I hit the lottery with you, Pop.

Heather Wilde - I don't even know where to begin. You have been instrumental in this project from its inception to publication. I couldn't ask for a better friend and co-adventurer along the way to bring *Hot Tub Mommy* into the world! You have encouraged me, grounded me, guided this project, and made me laugh countless times. Thank you for being you.

Chani Becker - thank you for your outstanding artistry and design skills. You brought the cover to life in a way I couldn't even have imagined! I'm so grateful for your energy, expertise, and artwork.

Lindsay Smith - thank you for working your magic once more! You are one of my very favorite humans and my first go-to when it comes to figuring out those pesky subtitles.

JoRie Antuña and & Lisette Bray - from the first conversation we had where I told you I was toying with the idea of starting my own business "someday" to your reassurances that I would, indeed, figure out at least a few parts of this whole motherhood thing, your confidence and support have meant the world. I'm so grateful for our friendship.

Rochelle Dailey - this book would not have happened without you and your incredible support. You have transformed my business, which has transformed my life. Your vigilance over my calendar and anticipation of things that would make life easier created the space for me to write. Thank you a million times over!

To the fabulous ladies of the brunch bunch/Scooter Squad - Edith Baltierrez, Brandi Flores, Kelsey Lamphier, and Danielle Osborne, thank you for fueling my progress with ridiculously overpriced breakfast beverages, edible glitter, tiny suitcases, and endless laughs. I'm so grateful for our friendships!

To the Misfit Birds crew: Heather Wilde, Jennifer Clark, Melissa Pratt, Sophie Lagacé, Carol Boruff, and Tracy Chaplin Meisterheim - thank you for the consistent and creative spaces we shared and for all the positive energy and encouragement.

Dr. Aubree Bennett - thank you for the amazing healing and energy work you provided along the way so I could stay in tip-top shape to get this book written. I'm so grateful for you and your amazing gifts!

Trisha Scamehorn and Alyssa Knodel - thank you for sharing your energy as beta readers. Your feedback and input was invaluable.

Jennie Jolly - your editing support was outstanding. Thank you for polishing up my words and helping this come to life!

Alison Kelley - thank you for being such a wonderfully magical part of my team! Your creativity and patience have added so much to my business. Thank you for always being such an incredible person to partner with.

Pam Davis - from text fests to shared memes to hot springs and mountain retreats, your friendship, encouragement, and excitement along the way meant the world!

Hillside Spot restaurant - a huge thank you to all the team members who served me countless times and always created a comfortable (and yummy!) environment. I'm so grateful you continued to stock pistachio syrup regardless of what season it was so I could enjoy my lattes. I'm pretty sure half this book was written at your establishment!

About the Author

Nicole Lance is an entrepreneur, proud mom and stepmom, happy partner to her husband Sean, and ignorer of laundry piles. When she's not cussing over the Lego bricks her daughter leaves scattered on the floor, you can find Nicole journaling and writing in her big, yellow chair, working with coaching clients, leading women's executive readiness workshops, facilitating with teams, and speaking at conferences. She is the author of *Awesome on Your Own Terms*, *Hot Tub Mommy*, and *Bold on the Inside*.

Connect with the Author

Nicolelance.co
Facebook.com/NicoleLanceCoaching
LinkedIn.com/in/nicolelance
Instagram.com/nicolelancecoaching

Leave a Review

If you enjoyed reading *Hot Tub Mommy*, would you consider leaving a review on a platform of your choice? Reviews help indie-published authors find more readers like you.

www.ingramcontent.com/pod-product-compliance
Lightning Source LLC
Chambersburg PA
CBHW070718130626
46553CB00005B/2042